THE S.P.E.A.R. METHOD

Enjoy the book!

Kuda

THE
S.P.E.A.R.
METHOD

5 SIMPLE STEPS TO BALANCED
SUCCESS AND FULFILLMENT

KUDA BIZA

NEW DEGREE PRESS

THE S.P.E.A.R. METHOD

5 Simple Steps to Balanced Success and Fulfillment

ISBN   978-1-64137-951-9   *Paperback*

         978-1-64137-765-2   *Kindle Ebook*

         978-1-64137-767-6   *Ebook*

To all the goal-getters pursuing both success and fulfillment.

CONTENTS

———

*"The three most important days in life are the day you are born, the day you find out why, and **each day you act on your why.**"*

—KUDA BIZA

INTRODUCTION

I was exhausted.

I'd spent the entire afternoon fishing in the bay and exploring Sarasota, Florida, with my friends Danene and Paul Jaffe. The sun's fatiguing power sent me straight to bed right after dinner at 8:00 p.m. Around 1:00 a.m., I was roused from a deep sleep by my phone vibrating on the nightstand. I was so tired, I thought about ignoring it, but something told me to resist that urge. I finally answered, right before I missed the call. Seeing the number was from Zimbabwe, my home country, I was suddenly wide awake. I hoped it wasn't a butt dial from my sister Miriam, who had a history of making that mistake.

I whispered hello so I wouldn't wake my wife, Ruth, who was sleeping next to me. This time, Miriam was on the other end of line crying. Hearing her cry, I immediately realized something terrible had happened. She took a minute to catch her breath and share the sad news: my eldest sister, Memory, had suddenly passed away. A wave of uncontrollable emotion welled up in me. I felt helpless and wanted nothing more than to be with my family, who were ten thousand miles away. I could only imagine how devastated my parents were—not to mention my three nieces, who had just lost their mother.

Memory's death came as a surprise to everyone. Things happened so quickly. A few days earlier, she had been attacked by a dog while walking with her husband and eighteen-month-old daughter, Kayla. After learning of the assault, the dog owner assured my sister that his dog was vaccinated. We later learned that was a lie. Not only had he given false testimony, but he also bribed a local veterinarian to corroborate his story. Memory and the local clinic believed the veterinarian, so they did not treat the wound beyond the basic wound dressing.

Unfortunately, the dog was rabid, and Memory contracted rabies. When rabies symptoms appeared two days later, she was taken to the hospital and learned it was too late to cure the infection. It had spread through her whole body. To make matters worse, the hospital had no vaccine available to at least try to save her life. My family ordered and airfreighted the vaccine from South Africa. By the time it arrived, her condition had deteriorated severely and the nurse on duty did not even bother to administer the vaccine. A few hours later, Memory died. A newspaper later reported that the same rabid dog attacked twenty-three people. Three had died, one of whom was my sister.[1]

---

1   Tinotenda Samukange, "Rabid Dog Leaves 3 Dead, 13 Injured," *News Day*, May 15, 2015.

The night I learned of her death, I was on the phone with Miriam for less than five minutes, but the call felt like an eternity. This moment was my first time receiving news of losing someone close to me. I spent the next hour or so in the dark in bed crying. At around 3:00 a.m., I finally composed myself, woke Ruth, and shared the news. We immediately packed our bags and quietly left our friends' house without any goodbye hugs.

The four-hour drive back home was quiet. Neither of us spoke. We were still processing what had happened. We arrived home right before 7:00 a.m. I called my parents, and we all cried together on the phone. I was not able to attend my sister's funeral in Zimbabwe, but I managed to make it to her memorial a few months later. At her memorial, countless thoughts and questions ran through my head. Questions like:

Did Memory achieve her lifelong dreams?
Was she fulfilled? Was she happy?
Did she achieve her life's purpose?

Perhaps you have lost a loved one. I suspect these are questions that came to your mind as well. You might even be thinking these questions about yourself.

HOW WILL YOUR STORY END?

When you get to the end of your own life, what do you want to look back and see? Sitting in your rocking chair on your front porch in your twilight years, what memories will you relive? Will you think of the amount of fame and fortune you made or how many Instagram likes you averaged each day? Or will you reflect on a life in which you achieved both success and fulfillment?

My sincere hope is that as you reflect on your life, a big smile will stretch across your face because you enjoyed a great sense of fulfillment and achieved success. When all is said and done, life's ultimate goal is for one to achieve success and fulfillment—a sense of internal joy, happiness, and contentment through a life well lived with zero regrets.

Author and entrepreneur Jesse Iztler said it best when I heard him speak at the Next Gen Summit in New York City. He described life as a ride on a bus: "You never know when the bus will arrive at your bus stop and when your life will end. So, while the bus is still moving, make the most of every single moment because with each passing moment you are getting closer and closer to your bus stop."

My sister's passing made me realize tomorrow is never guaranteed. We need to approach each day with a sense of urgency, as if our life's bus could stop at any second. By having such a mindset and by treating every single day as your last, you can't help but take immediate massive action in your quest to achieve success and fulfillment in whatever you decide to do.

Undoubtedly, the loss of my sister changed me in more ways than you can imagine. It made me think beyond just achieving success. I wanted to make sure whatever I did would give me ultimate fulfillment. Life is too short to not be happy, successful, and fulfilled. As a matter of fact, this loss was one of the main reasons I decided to write this book.

You see, many people wait until they are famous or have achieved big success before they muster up the courage to write a book. Although I see tremendous wisdom in waiting for the right time, because tomorrow is never guaranteed, I am sharing my experiences now. My life is fulfilled when I give to others, and this book gives valuable insight that will hopefully change your life in a positive way.

MY BUS RIDE

My bus ride so far has been interesting and entailed its fair share of successes, failures, and lessons. I like to tell people I have taken the scenic route from the vibrant streets of sub-Saharan Africa to the luscious beaches of South Florida to, more recently, the hustle and bustle of Manhattan. I cannot wait to see where it goes next.

However, I will admit that, for most of my life, my bus ride has been solely about achieving success. But my sister's passing ushered in a new perspective, one in which I would seek for more balance in my life: a pursuit of success, greater impact on the world, and the attainment of personal fulfillment.

This new perspective has led me to venture on a quest to find how one can achieve balanced success and fulfillment. This journey has led to the discovery of the S.P.E.A.R. method, a framework I believe will help you achieve both success and fulfillment in your own life so when you eventually sit in that rocking chair reflecting on your life, you won't want to trade a single second of it.

THE S.P.E.A.R. METHOD

For centuries, the *spear* has been the go-to tool when you want to hit a target. Ancient communities relied on the spear for protection during warfare and to bring food to the table when they went hunting. What I like about the spear is its simplicity in design yet extreme efficacy. The same is true about the S.P.E.A.R method—simple yet effective.

You may be wondering what the acronym S.P.E.A.R stands for:

- **Seek your why.**
- **Plan.**
- **Execute.**
- **Achieve.**
- **Repeat.**

The book is written in five parts, each corresponding a letter of the S.P.E.A.R method:

1. **SEEK YOUR WHY:** Gaining clarity on your life's purpose—your "why" is the first step in achieving success and fulfillment. Knowing your why will provide you with the direction you need to take your life. Before launching any spear, you must aim in your desired direction.
2. **PLAN:** As they say, failing to plan is planning to fail. Once you know your life's purpose, creating a plan to achieve that purpose is essential. Planning is the equivalent of sharpening the spearhead so you can pierce your target. You need to know how to break down your purpose into short-term goals and develop your plan of attack to achieve these goals.

3. **EXECUTE:** If you know your why and create a plan but never execute that plan, you are almost guaranteed to never achieve the success and attain the fulfillment you seek. The three most important days in your life are the day you are born, the day you find your why, and each day you take action toward your why. Taking action is the thrust you give your spear as you launch it. The more action you take, the more velocity (and force) your spear has. Since achieving success and fulfillment will require stepping outside your comfort zone, you need to know how to form habits that make you become comfortable with the uncomfortable.

4. **ACHIEVE:** The first, and probably most important, achievement is when you take that first step outside your comfort zone. However, you may experience many of life's twist and turns as you venture toward success, which means your attitude will determine your altitude.

5. **REPEAT:** Once you achieve a goal that's part of your life's purpose, you are set to repeat the process on the next goal. Goals are the oxygen of your dreams. They are how you keep the dream alive. Pick up your spear and go find your next hunt.

The final chapters of this book were completed during the COVID-19 global pandemic. Life has changed quite a bit since I started working on this book. Right now, close to three million people worldwide have confirmed cases of COVID-19, with almost certainty of more cases to come.[2] On May 1, 2020, the US government released figures showing that

---

2   Maria Cohut, "COVID-19 Global Impact: How the Coronavirus Is Affecting the World," *Medical News Today*, April 24, 2020.

the pandemic erased 20.5 million jobs and sent the nation's unemployment rate to 14.7 percent, the highest since at least the 1940s.[3]

The pandemic has been disruptive to almost everyone on Earth, and life as we knew it may never be the same again. If there were ever a time to master the S.P.E.A.R method, it is now. Going forward, the need for a framework that will help you establish habits for success, unlock your potential to impact the world in a way that only you can, and attain your own personal fulfillment is needed more than ever before. I highly recommend that you start implementing this information in your life today. I've spent over five years refining this concept, and I am excited to share it with you now.

---

3   Don Lee, "Unemployment Hits 14.7% in April. How Long before 20.5 Million Lost Jobs Come Back?" *LA Times*, May 8, 2020.

PART ONE

SEEK YOUR WHY

CHAPTER 1

SEEK YOUR WHY

___

Your purpose in life is to find your purpose and give your whole heart and soul to it.

—BUDDHA

In December 2018, my wife, Ruth, and I decided to spend the holidays with my sister Martha and her family in Cambridge, England. The last time we had seen them was at our wedding in Florida, more than a year prior. We were looking forward to spending quality time with our toddler nephew and niece, Myles and Hannah. At the wedding, Myles was only a year and a half and Hannah was just two months old. A few days in, I was amazed (and drained) by Myles's curiosity. He was going through the "why" phase, and when he was around, you would be lucky to get five seconds of peace and quiet.

"Uncle, why is your shirt blue?"
"Why are you brushing your teeth?"
"Why are you watching TV?"

Each answer to his question would be followed by another why. Answer that question and you get another why. And another and another and another. The questions would go on and on and on. At times, conversation with Myles felt like an FBI interrogation, but the cute, innocent version. I soon realized Myles was not doing this to be annoying. In fact, he was just trying to better understand the world around him and how to best navigate it.

This experience also made me ponder whether we tend to take things for granted and lose that art of asking "why" as we get older. How many people clearly understand their why and have a greater sense of their life's purpose?

THE GOLDEN CIRCLE

One of the most popular TED Talks ever given, "Start with Why" by bestselling author Simon Sinek (which is also the title of his book), introduces the concept of the Golden Circle: a diagram of a bullseye with "Why" in the innermost circle, surrounded by a ring labeled "How," enclosed in a ring labeled "What."

- **Why:** your purpose, the reason you exist.
- **How:** the processes and methods used to fulfill the purpose.
- **What:** the results and outcomes.

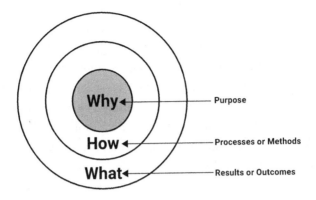

Figure 1.1

Sinek argues that we should go from the inside out of the circle, meaning we should start by clearly understanding our why. When we have clarity about our purpose, determining the processes and desired outcomes becomes much easier.

After interviewing over four thousand of the world's most influential leaders, author Corey Poirier was able to conclude that your why matters. His findings made clear that the most common attribute these leaders possessed was a strong sense of clarity around their true purpose, and their actions are focused around supporting that why.[4]

HITTING THE BULLSEYE
Hitting the bullseye (the "Why" in the Golden Circle) requires a tool you can throw straight at your target—like a spear. Throughout human history, spears have been used

4   Corey Poirier, "Why Your 'Why' Matters," *Forbes*, October 31, 2017.

both for hunting and warfare. In southern Africa, where I grew up, spears were the principle weapon, with different types of spears used for battles, hunting, and even fishing.[5] While hunting, spears give the hunter a unique advantage to kill their prey from a distance, which is especially important considering the same prey is being hunted by predators like lions, cheetahs, and leopards. Having a tool that allows a hunter to hit the target from a safe hidden spot some yards away was game-changing.

Still an effective form of weaponry even in this modern age, the spear has largely remained the same over time. Not only has the physical spear stood the test of time, but so too has the figurative spear, which holds the namesake of my life method, S.P.E.A.R.

The S in the S.P.E.A.R. method stands for **seek**. For you to achieve success and ultimately attain fulfillment, you first must **seek and understand your life's purpose and calling**—your why. Your life's purpose acts as a GPS to guide you to the goals you will set for yourself, and the actions you will take in your quest to a fulfilling life. So the pressing question becomes: how do you determine your life's purpose?

I will be the first to admit that finding your life's purpose is not easy, and no foolproof exercise exists that guarantees you will discover it. However, you can take certain steps that may lead you there or at the very least get you quite close. For a long time, I struggled to clearly articulate my life's

---

5   "Weapons of Southern Africa," National Museum Publications, accessed May 24, 2020.

purpose. I was only able to fully grasp it after working with Rich Keller, a motivational speaker and personal branding expert. A graduate of the Wharton School of the University of Pennsylvania, Rich pursued an adventurous corporate career with brands like Godiva and Chips Ahoy! After Rich overcome cancer at age twenty-six, he found his why. He'd spent years in the corporate world but had always wanted to help young adults uncover their unique power. He resigned from his job and started Catalyst Branding Foundations, a company dedicated to discovering your core value. He developed a process to get the core of who you are down to one word. His word is CATALYST, and he lives every letter of it.

When we started working together, Rich asked me to send an email to five people who knew me best. I asked them all one question: "What makes me unique?" All seven of my respondents (yes, I overdelivered) named similar qualities— my focus on entrepreneurship, social impact, and empowerment. This consistent feedback helped me understand myself better, and I gained clarity on my calling. Having insight from others gives you a better sense of how to leverage your uniqueness and deliver value to the world.

If you do not know your purpose, consider reaching out to about five (or seven) people who know you well and ask them what makes you unique.

If you already have a sense of your life's purpose, I encourage you to do the exercise anyway. You may uncover a few strengths or reaffirm what you already know. Either way, you'll eliminate self-doubt.

The more self-aware you are, the better. Asking soul-searching questions is the first step to recognizing your why—your life's purpose. You will be surprised to learn you already know the answers to what you seek.

QUESTIONS YOU CAN ASK YOURSELF TO HELP YOU FIND YOUR PURPOSE:

- What excites me?
- When am I most comfortable?
- What am I willing to make sacrifices for?
- Which of my traits and attributes tend to stand out the most?
- What do others say I am meant to do with my life?
- Where do I find the most inspiration?
- With a year to live, what would I spend most of time working on?
- Where could I provide the most value to others?
- But don't stop there. Seeking your purpose takes time and, more importantly, curiosity.

CHAPTER 2

CURIOSITY AWAKENED THE LION

———

I have no special talent. I am only passionately curious.

—ALBERT EINSTEIN

If most kids were to get $20 from their grandmother, spending it on toys or treats would be at the top of their list of what to do with the money (the younger me would have spent it on ice cream). But not if you are Joshua Williams. Growing up in South Florida from a family of Jamaican descent, Joshua received $20 as a gift from his grandmother. On his way to church, he saw a homeless man begging for help with a sign that said, "Need Food, Lost My Job." In that moment, Joshua immediately knew what he had to do. The four-and-half-year-old boy gave this man the $20 he had just been given. Joshua had concluded that this man desperately needed the money more than he did.

A few weeks later, Joshua saw a commercial on TV about children suffering from hunger. He remembered the homeless man and wondered why this problem was happening. Many children his age would have been more concerned with toys and playing games, but these two events triggered a curiosity in Joshua to find a solution to end hunger. Joshua convinced his mother to start cooking Jamaican food for struggling people in their neighborhood over the weekends as way to help end the crisis.

At first, about five people would show up to collect the meals. In two months, word had spread and about fifteen people were coming regularly for the weekend meals. A year later, they were giving food to about two hundred people every weekend. Joshua and his family were pretty much footing the bill for all these meals.

With help from his family, Joshua, now seven years old, launched Joshua's Heart Foundation (JHF), a 501(c)(3) not-for-profit organization dedicated to the fight against global hunger and poverty. Founded in 2005, JHF also engages and educates young people to fight hunger and poverty on a global basis. The organization is youth-run and has attracted partnerships from corporations such as Whole Foods Market, Unilever, Walmart, Publix, and T.J. Maxx.

As of this writing, JHF has raised over $1 million to stomp out hunger, distributed over 2.2 million pounds of food, recruited over twenty-five thousand youth volunteers, assisted over four hundred twenty thousand individuals, and served more than half a million meals to families in the Miami area and beyond. In 2012, Joshua became the youngest recipient of the White House's Champions of Change Award, an Obama administration honor that recognized individuals doing extraordinary things to make a difference in their communities.[6] Joshua is now a sophomore at New York University (NYU) and admits that the day he became curious about how to solve hunger was the day he found his life's purpose.

My favorite Merriam-Webster definition for curiosity is "a strong desire to know or learn something."[7] The best way to find your purpose is to be curious and have a strong desire to learn about yourself. Increasing your self-awareness will most likely lead you to find your purpose. Curious people tend to ask questions in their search for answers, which can ignite discovery. Asking questions like "Who am I?" and "What do I want to do with my life?" can help you gain clarity on what is meaningful to you.

I am naturally curious. When I was in fourth grade, my older sister Miriam and I used to walk two miles every day to school and then take the bus home after. The walk to school was somewhat predictable. It was like experiencing déjà vu every morning. We saw the same group of kids wearing the same Hatfield Primary School uniform chasing each other on their way to school. Mr. Stephens, the owner of the local grocery store, would always be outside his store setting up for the day. The herd of people was waiting at the shopping center bus stop on their way to work. The same blue Nissan Sentra would drive past us, usually by the police station.

---

6   "Champions of Change—Joshua Williams," The White House, accessed on January 23, 2020.

7   *Merriam-Webster*, s.v. "curiosity (_n._)," accessed April 6, 2020.

Then there was that group of kids playing in their front yard in their pajamas, showing no sign they were planning to go to school. Each day we would walk past their house wondering why they did not attend school; I figured they were home-schooled. During the winters I envied them because they did not have to deal with a two-mile walk at 6:00 a.m.

I was curious to find out what was going on, especially since everyone did not want to associate with them for some odd reason. I remember one time I overheard a group of women walking in front of us gossiping that the family was cursed, and that one should stay away from them or else they as well would be cursed.

I could not stop wondering, *Who cursed them? And why? Why do the kids not go to school?* These were all the questions that ran through my head each time I walked past their house.

I decided to investigate this mysterious group of kids to learn the real story. After school one day, I intentionally missed the bus home so I could walk home alone. I did not tell anyone, not even Miriam, about my plan, because I was worried she would object. Also, I was afraid that if I told anyone about my plan, I would be deemed cursed as well.

When I entered their yard and started making my way to the patio where the kids were, my heart started pounding so hard. I began to think, *What if the stories of the curse are true?* I tried to talk myself out of the idea and leave, but it was too late. Right before I could turn back, one of the kids started running to me and shouted, "Hi, I am Sara! What's your name? Are you here to play with us?"

I froze for a moment before responding, "My name is Kuda. Yes, I can play."

The entire group was excited that someone new came to play. Sara was the same age as me and the eldest of the bunch. The next two hours flew by without my even noticing. Sara and her three siblings—Michael, Jessica, and Linda—did not have any toys but used their imaginations to great effect to make playtime fun. Instead of a toy car, we used bricks as our cars, and we would drag these bricks in the sand, imagining we were driving Formula 1 cars.

When the time came for me to head home, I realized I had almost forgotten my "mission." I asked Sara, "Where do you guys go to school?" A brief silence ensued before she replied, visibly embarrassed, "We do not go to school. Our grandma cannot afford to pay for us to attend."

Sara explained that her grandmother was retired and did not have a source of income to pay the fees for her orphan grandchildren. All she could provide them was shelter and food, nothing more.

At that time, primary school education in Zimbabwe was no longer free. So if you were in Sara's situation, with no breadwinner who can pay the fees, you would not attend school. Her reply was an answer I did not expect, so to make the situation less awkward, I went on to ask, "So what do you want to be when you grow up?"

Sara looked me straight in the eyes, with a confused look on her face. She replied, "Both my parents are dead. I do not attend school; I am just waiting to die."

Hearing those words coming out of a nine-year-old girl sent this sharp chill down my spine. I did not know what to say next. I was in a state of total shock. Usually when I asked that question, other kids would reply with "I want to be a pilot" or "a doctor" or "a lawyer." Sara had concluded that since both her parents had passed and she was not getting an education, dreaming of a brighter future was pointless.

I said my goodbyes and headed home. On my walk home I wondered why the community or the government was not paying Sara's tuition fees. Before I arrived home that day, I made a promise to myself that I was going to find a way to make education more available to those who do not have access to it. This promise became my life's purpose. Although I was just in fourth grade, I was determined to play my part in changing the world; I just was not sure how yet. That day, curiosity did not kill the cat but instead awakened the lion.

As I reflect even now, this conversation marked a defining day in my life. Through that experience, I made it my mission to use my talents, knowledge, and skills to do good for humanity by giving a fighting chance to people who need it. By being curious, I awoke to a greater calling that has given me greater meaning and context, which is why I try to make sure every entrepreneurial venture I have cofounded has a social mission. Here is what I have been able to do so far:

- **AFR Clothing:** Launched in 2009, while I was a senior in college, this socially conscious apparel brand donates 20 percent of profits to educate children in need in Africa. To date, we have paid for the education of hundreds of children Ghana, Tanzania, and Zimbabwe.
- **#ThisIsMyEra:** Launched in 2014, #ThisIsMyEra is a personal development brand that provides people with tools to help them accomplish their goals. For every #ThisIsMyEra 90-day planner sold, #ThisIsMyEra donates a stationary kit to students in need.
- **Wakami Arabia:** In 2014, Wakami Arabia started distributing a line of handmade bracelets in Saudi Arabia. We are empowering and improving the livelihoods of rural women in Guatemala who make the bracelets.
- **Signables:** Launched in 2018, Signables offers a line of officially licensed sports merchandise. We have partnered with LEAD Africa to provide scholarships to send student-athletes to their academies in Africa.
- **Nunbelievable:** Launched in 2019, Nunbelievable is a mission-based baked goods company combatting hunger in the United States by donating a meal for every cookie we sell.

In fact, I am donating 10 percent of proceeds from this book's sales toward a scholarship fund that educates underprivileged children in Zimbabwe through the Amani Hope Foundation, a nonprofit organization I founded. In 2016, UNESCO Institute for Statistics (UIS) reported that about 263 million children and youth who were supposed to be enrolled in school were out of school. This number is equivalent to more than a quarter of the population of Europe and 80 percent of the population of the United States.[8]

I still hear Sara's words in my mind as if that day were yesterday. I acknowledge how fortunate I am to have an education, which is why I give education as a gift to others through my nonprofit, the Amani Hope Foundation. As Nelson Mandela once said, "Education is the most powerful weapon which you can use to change the world." Giving others education is my way of changing the world.

How can you leverage curiosity in finding your purpose? Without clarity on what your life's purpose is, you will have extreme difficulty finding fulfillment, which is why **seeking your purpose** is the first step of the S.P.E.A.R. method. Once you know your purpose, you can aim your spear in the right direction and then be ready to launch it into flight.

Now you know that finding your purpose is the first step in attaining true happiness and fulfillment in your life. Once you have clarity in what your purpose is, the next step in the S.P.E.A.R. method is "P," which stands for **plan**. Having a plan of attack is essential if you want to entertain any hopes of achieving your life's purpose and goals. You must know why planning is important, how to create a plan, and how you can make planning a daily ritual.

---

8   "263 Million Children and Youth Are out of School | UNESCO UIS," UNESCO, accessed on January 22, 2020.

PART TWO

PLAN

CHAPTER 3

EVERY FLIGHT NEEDS A FLIGHT PLAN

For tomorrow belongs to the people who prepare for it today.
—AFRICAN PROVERB

Each time I board an airplane, I always peek into the cockpit. I know I am not the only one who does that. My friend Liran Hirschkorn takes it a step further and always asks the pilots to take a selfie with him in the cockpit. For me, I just like to see that the pilots are busy working on their flight plan as they prepare for takeoff. It gives me peace of mind for the flight.

In college, I studied business and aviation for my undergraduate degree. In my aviation classes, I learned the importance of creating a flight plan prior to a flight. A flight plan typically contains important information, like the route the flight intends to take, departure and arrival points, cruising altitude, estimated time en route, and alternate airports in case of bad weather, among other factors. It maps out the path the pilot intends to take to get to their destination.

Imagine the havoc and pandemonium that would occur if pilots did not take the time to plan their flight and instead just hopped into the cockpit and winged it (no pun intended).

In life, many people do exactly that: they just wing it. They never take the time to create a plan on how they intend to arrive at their desired destination. Some do not even take the time to figure out what their destination is in the first place.

A 2017 survey showed that only one-third of Americans have a life plan they have committed to in writing and use to help guide them through the rest of their lives.[9] This statistic is shocking, to say the least. Based on the 2018 US Census Bureau data, this number would mean that 171 million Americans over the age of eighteen do not have a life plan in place. Now, I don't know about you, but I certainly do not want to be part of that group.

A wedding planner I met once jokingly said that some people spend more time planning their wedding than they do planning the rest of their lives. It's sad to think more time and effort are spent in planning one day than all the others.

Your life is so important that you cannot afford to just wing it and be a passenger. You must be the captain pilot and take control. As the pilot of your own life, you need to invest time

---

9   "Survey Finds Two-Thirds of Americans Do Not Have a Plan for Their Life," PR Newswire, accessed on March 7, 2020.

in creating your own "flight" plan, which is why the second step of the S.P.E.A.R. method is **plan**. After taking the time and effort to become self-aware and seek your goals in life, you must invest some time planning how you will achieve these goals.

Stephen Covey, author of the popular book *The 7 Habits of Highly Effective People*, said, "Make time for planning; wars are won in the general's tent." You want to make sure each day you step out on the battlefield, spear in hand, ready to fight whatever life throws at you with a plan in place on how you are going to win war.

HOW IMPORTANT ARE PLANS?

Imagine trying to build the house of your dreams without any architectural blueprint.

How about a team attempting to win the Super Bowl with no plan whatsoever on how it will defend and run offense against its opponent?

Or someone trying to raise capital for a business without a plan to show potential investors?

Since achieving your life's purpose is uncharted territory, developing a plan on how you are going to get to your goal is critical. The same way an architectural blueprint gives a builder direction on what they need to build, having a plan on how you aim to achieve your life's purpose is your blueprint to reach your North Star.

Since nothing in life is guaranteed, having a plan does not guarantee you success. However, having this roadmap does increase your chances of success. A 2010 study found that companies that plan grow 30 percent faster than those that do not. The same study also found that businesses with a plan grew faster and were more successful than those that did not plan.[10] How do plans do that? A plan outlines the specific actions you need to take and when in order to reach certain milestones as you work toward achieving your goals. Without an outline of the specific actions you need to take, you can easily find yourself distracted and overwhelmed.

To help our customers learn firsthand from successful people from many walks of life, we launched the #ThisIsMyEra podcast, cohosted by myself and my close friend and business partner, Alexander Star. We got the privilege of interviewing self-made millionaires, professional athletes, artists, social entrepreneurs, and more. We found successful people all agreed that having a plan in place played a key role in their success since it helped them focus on the task at hand. A plan provided them with a road map that ultimately helped them achieve their goal.

Drs. Travis and Jenna Zigler, founders of Eye Love, a company that sells high-quality, affordable products supporting eye health, credit planning as the key driver of their success. The first step they took was writing down what they call a "vivid vision" for Eye Love, following the vivid vision planning framework developed by author and entrepreneur

10   A. Burke, S. Fraser, & F.J. Greene. "The Multiple Effects of Business Planning on New Venture Performance," *Journal of Management Studies*, 47(3) May 2010: 391-415.

Cameron Herold. Their vivid vision includes short-term and long-term goals, with metrics to measure success. By taking time to do this planning exercise, they were able to articulate Eye Love's mission and expand it into a robust road map they reference daily as they grow their business.[11] Their vivid vision has helped them stay on track toward their goals and grow their business into a multimillion-dollar empire. They even use their vivid vision to find the right talent for their team. Their success has enabled them to change lives by giving a portion of profits to provide eye care to people in developing countries like Ecuador and Jamaica.

PLAN FOR ALL AREAS OF LIFE

I am a husband, son, brother, uncle, nephew, friend, entrepreneur, investor, author, business partner, speaker, philanthropist, and runner, and one day I will be a father. We all wear different hats daily. Obviously some hats take priority over others, but we need to make sure that during the time we are wearing a specific hat, we have clarity and meaning on what we need to do to achieve success and fulfillment. So take time to plan for the different areas of life that are important to you.

Doing so helps you not only have clear direction for where you need to go, but also prioritize among all these different areas. Depending on your life's season, you may find yourself focusing more on one area of life, leaving the other areas neglected and your life off-balance. Although this setup can

---

11 Travis and Jenna Zigler, "Creating A Vivid Vision," July 27, 2018, in *ThisIsMyEra the Podcast*. Produced by Kuda Biza and Alexander Star, podcast, MP3 audio, 44:04.

be sustainable for short seasons, prolonged periods with your life off-balance will certainly hurt your ability to attain fulfillment. Just as financial advisers rebalance a portfolio periodically, you need a process to rebalance your life regularly.

The Wheel of Life is a tool that can help you evaluate how balanced your life is and create a comprehensive plan for your life. I first found out about the Wheel of Life tool through an executive coaching program with Success Motivation Institute (SMI). The Wheel of Life is split into sections, with each section representing a different area of your life. The sections of the wheel can be changed to suit your personal vision of what a meaningful and balanced life looks like. Here is a list of common areas to get you started.

1. **Family:** your relationship with your family.
2. **Health:** your physical and emotional well-being.
3. **Career/Entrepreneurial:** your job/work that earns money.
4. **Financial:** your savings, investments, debt, etc.
5. **Personal Development:** time and resources spend on self-improvement.
6. **Spirituality:** your spiritual well-being.
7. **Social:** your relationships with other people, e.g., your friends.
8. **Contribution:** how you are making a difference and giving back.

If you would like to create your own Wheel of Life, you can fill out a free template on *www.SPEARMethod.com/resources.*

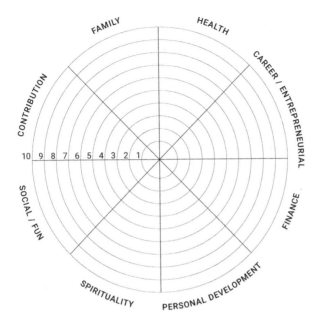

Figure 3.1

To create your Wheel of Life:

1. Identify the areas of life you want to use for the exercise. You may use the list I shared above to start.
2. Rank each area of life by the level of satisfaction with that area, with ten being extremely satisfied and zero being extremely dissatisfied.

If your life is fully in balance, your Wheel of Life will look like the one on the left—a perfect circle. If you're like most people, however, your Wheel of Life will look something like the one on the right—a wheel that is off-balance. For each of the areas that did not score a ten, especially the weakest, determine two to three actions you can take within the next thirty to ninety days to make improvements.

Done regularly, this exercise is excellent to help you identify where you are expending energy in your life and areas you may be neglecting. After identifying what your current energy dispersion looks like, the wheel can be used periodically throughout the year to reassess your progress in cultivating a balanced life.

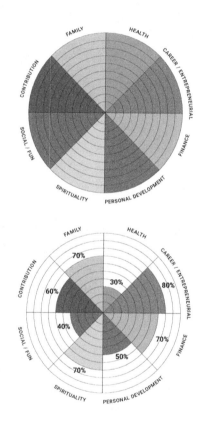

Figure 3.2

PLANNING CAN MAKE THE IMPROBABLE POSSIBLE

A few months after moving to New Jersey from Florida, I noticed I was not feeling my usual self. Something just wasn't right. I decided to do some self-reflection and dig in. I did the Wheel of Life exercise and noticed that my level of satisfaction with my health and fitness was remarkably low. My Wheel of Life was way off-balance. For a person who works out regularly, this revelation came as a surprise.

It dawned on me that I really missed exercising outdoors. Since the winters in New Jersey are much colder than Florida winters, I was forced to use the treadmill, which I hate. This change was making my workouts less enjoyable, so I kept making lame excuses to skip days.

The thought of spending four more months without any outdoor activity was horrifying. When someone suggested I take up skiing, I was aghast. This sport seemed impossible to conquer in my mind. Having grown up in Zimbabwe, a country that does not get any snow, and then spending twelve years in sunny Florida, winter sports like skiing were as foreign as a jockey attempting a career in sumo wrestling. I felt like I was being asked to go outside and slay Goliath.

Still, as I wrote down the actions I had to take in the next ninety days to improve my health and fitness area of life, I knew a winter sport was necessary. Fortunately, over the years I have learned to condition myself to never negotiate with my goals. I pushed myself to take up skiing so I could rebalance my Wheel of Life and not compromise my fitness goals.

Once I got to the slopes, my fears of winter sports were justified. Within five minutes, I had made the bold yet foolish move of trying to "wing it." That first day at the ski resort, I felt lucky to not have ended up in the hospital with broken bones. I fell to the ground every time I started moving forward. For those around me, the experience was like seeing a baby learn to walk. Each time I started moving, I would lean back (and not forward), which guarantees you'll fall flat on your back. Humbled and defeated, I remember sitting at dinner gazing at the slopes thinking, *I will conquer you soon, but first I need to go back to the basics; I have to create a plan.*

That night, I created my plan: I'd spend the evening watching YouTube videos on how to ski. Then, the next day, I would sign up for beginner ski lessons from 8:00 a.m. to 12:00 p.m. Then I'd practice the rest of day after my lunch break. I knew one session with the coach was a good start, but not enough. I planned to come out on the slopes every other weekend that winter to practice after each lesson. This plan helped me become a much better skier and ensured that I stayed on track with my fitness goal. Although I am not riding black diamond ski slopes yet, I fall far less than before, and each winter, I cannot wait to go out on the slopes. My fear of winter sports has turned into a love affair. And what seemed impossible is now a piece of cake.

At times, a simple plan is all you need to get you to your goal, but without it you may never cross that bridge to make your goal become your new reality. This simple plan helped me succeed in my skiing quest:

3. **First, I had to SEEK my why:** When I decided to start skiing, I had clarity on why this was something important. Since I had already done the process of seeking my why, I had set clear health and fitness goals. I knew I needed to find an outdoor physical activity during the winter months that would replace my outdoor running. I encountered moments when I wanted to give up, but I clearly understood the purpose, which helped me stay motivated and get up each time I fell on the ground.

4. **Second, I let a process be my PLAN:** When you are starting something new, like a Zimbabwean trying to ski, you must leverage a tried and tested process that you can follow to accelerate the learning curve. As you are developing your plan, do your research to see if someone has created processes you can include in your plan to help you get to where you want to go quicker. You can always make improvements to the existing process to make it your own, but following an existing method accelerates the process and may even reduce the number of mistakes you will make. Working with a coach, a mentor, or someone who can guide you will speed up the process, which is why even elite athletes, entrepreneurs, and heads of state have coaches and mentors. When I learned to ski, my process was simple: I hired a coach who had a process for beginners learning how to ski.

5. **Third, I EXECUTED my plan:** After creating my plan, I took action. I watched the YouTube videos, bought the necessary gear, and spent hours on the slopes working on my plan.

6. **Fourth, I ACHIEVED my goal:** After executing my plan, I was able to ski much better and no longer fall

embarrassingly. More importantly, I was able to do a sport that allowed me to work out in the outdoors during the winter.

7. **Lastly, I REPEATED what I'd learned:** Bruce Lee said it best when he said, "I fear not the man who has practiced 10,000 kicks once, but I fear the man who has practiced one kick 10,000 times." Ever try to learn a new language or skill? The key to mastering that skill is practice. When I started learning how to ski, I did not give up after the first day, even though the falls were painful. I went back out again and again. Each time I went out, before learning something new, I would first practice the things that I had learned thus far. Through repetition, I was able to master this new skill. Remember the words of Zig Ziglar: "repetition is the mother of learning."

MYTH: PLANS ARE STATIC

One of the misconceptions about planning I once heard is that when you create a plan, it's locked and can't be changed. A plan is not supposed to be static. You are not supposed to lock it up in the safe and never look at it again after you create it. If you do so, you are doomed.

I am of the opinion that plans are meant to be dynamic and fluid. You need to constantly review and modify your plan based on any new information you gather as you make progress toward the achievement of your goal.

Ideally, the target (your goal/life's purpose) should remain constant, but the plan, as well as the subsequent actions you take to hit the target, should change depending on circumstances. Think of your plan as your tactical missile. Once it locks in its target and is launched, it will make the necessary adjustments in its trajectory to hit the target. That is why basketball or football coaches like to call a time-out during the games. As the game situation changes, the game plan also changes—so having the flexibility to adjust the plan is key to claiming that victory.

Nothing can reinforce this idea of adjusting your plan in the wake of new circumstances better than what we have witnessed during the 2020 COVID-19 pandemic. I would like to even go as far as arguing that adaptability is probably the biggest lesson we can all take from the pandemic.

Remember, you must plan for all areas of life and leave room for changes, which is why you need a system to help you stay on track with all of your life goals while staying open to any opportunities.

CHAPTER 4

PREPARE FOR TAKEOFF

Give me six hours to chop down a tree and I will spend the first four sharpening the ax.

—ABRAHAM LINCOLN

History has taught us that if you do not innovate, you die. Look at companies like Blockbuster and Kodak, which were titans in their heydays but failed to constantly improve their offerings and anticipate the future. They went out of business. In fact, 88 percent of companies that were on the Fortune 500 list in 1955 were gone by 2014.[12] The same is true for individuals. To achieve your goals and life's potential, you need to constantly work on growing and improving yourself daily. The only way individuals grow is by having a good flywheel in place that sees them set a goal, develop a plan, take necessary action, analyze results, and make the necessary adjustments until they achieve their goal.

---

12   Mark Perry, "Fortune 500 firms in 1955 vs. 2014; 88% are gone, and we're all better off because of that dynamic 'creative destruction,'" *AEI* (blog), August 18, 2014.

In 2010, when I finished my MBA, I was fortunate enough to get hired by a Fortune 500 firm. The US economy had just gone through the 2008 financial crisis due to the subprime mortgage bubble, so getting a job straight out of college was a blessing. The firm that hired me had just created an innovation division, and the role I was hired for was new. Our small team of four was chartered with the task of creating new disruptive businesses that would help secure a bright future for this multibillion-dollar company. We were to take abstract ideas and turn them into practical business ventures that had revenue potential of at least $100 million within five years of launch. Thus, I had to find a way to improve myself, and learning how to be effective at planning and managing my time became my highest priority.

Back then, I was reading a book by Moky Makura called *Africa's Greatest Entrepreneurs*, which chronicles the journey of sixteen successful African entrepreneurs like Strive Masiyiwa and Mo Ibrahim. I read the story of Nigel Chanakira, a successful Zimbabwean banker and founder of Kingdom Financial Holdings, who talked about how he enrolled in a twelve-week program with Success Motivation Institute (SMI) that changed his life.[13] Nigel's bank had just experienced a bad second year in business, and he knew the best way he could save the bank was by first focusing on improving himself.

He credited his success with his bank and in life overall to this course. Obviously, I was intrigued and wanted to learn more. It just so happened that Nigel's cousin, Teurai Chanakira, was

---

13 Moky Makura, "Nigel Chanakira—The Wonder Boy Entrepreneur," *Africa's Greatest Entrepreneurs*, (Cape Town: Penguin), 142–60.

the very first model for AFR Clothing, a socially conscious brand I had started in college. I reached out to her to see if she could introduce me to Nigel, as I wanted to learn more about SMI and tips on how to plan and manage time better directly from the source.

A few days later, Nigel and I were on a Skype call. The first question he asked on the call is one I will never forget. He said, "Kuda, what is the largest room in life?"

I was not sure what he meant. Was he referring to an actual physical room in a building or something more philosophical?

So I answered, "I have the feeling you are about to tell me."

He responded, "The largest room in life is the room for improvement."

Like it or not, we all have room for improvement in all areas of life. But if we do not consistently take stock and create plans on how we are going to make these improvements, we will not make the most of the opportunity we get each day to improve. During the call, Nigel shared how he takes time to plan before starting each day. This act helps him stay centered and focused on his top priorities and goals. He also shared details about SMI and how he had worked with an executive coach there to help him get started in the process.

After the call, I signed up to learn more about the program. Randomly, I was matched up with same executive coach Nigel worked with almost twenty years ago—Ian Dawson. Talk about serendipity.

After taking the program, I saw massive improvements in my productivity, time management, and planning, as if I now had a compass showing me the way to my desired destination.

I felt a pressing urge to find a way to pass along this information to more people. Although I liked the SMI process, it was a little cumbersome and expensive. Without the coaching, it would be hard for someone to do. I went on an arduous search to find a planning system that was simple, effective, and affordable—one that allowed you to flexibly set long-term goals with the ability to break those goals into shorter milestones with a focus on all areas of life. By focusing on all areas of life, one could achieve balanced success and fulfillment. Over a five-year period, I tried close to twenty different planning systems to see which one was the best. All of them had their pros and cons, but ultimately, I decided to create my own.

After months of designing our planner, my wife and I finally had a prototype we were able to share with friends and family to try out. After getting feedback from our beta users, we refined the planner and took it to market. We launched the #ThisIsMyEra 90-day planner in September 2017, and as of this writing, we have sold tens of thousands of planners in the United States, Canada, Europe, and Australia.

What I love about the planner is that it has helped thousands of people plan their lives, master time management, increase their productivity, and ultimately achieve happiness. More importantly, with our buy-one, give-one model, we have been able to donate thousands of stationary kits to children in Zimbabwe and Tanzania, which gives us much joy and fulfillment.

PLANNING PROCESS

The #ThisIsMyEra 90-day planner is laid out in a way that makes the planning process easy. This product is a ninety-day planner because you have to be accountable to your long-range goals, but in smaller chunks, so you can actually see an end in sight. Having a ninety-day timeline lets you reset quicker than you could if you had to wait an entire year. The planner is laid out in way that allows you to

- **Develop Your Life Vision:** Write your life vision for all areas of your life as well as your life's purpose.
- **Master Your Goals:** Capture the goals you want to achieve in your lifetime that align with your vision. You should plan to set a master goal for each area of your life. For example, when it comes to contribution, if your vision is to impact lives by providing education, perhaps your lifetime goal is to send one million children to school through scholarships. Establishing this North Star helps provide clarity on what you want to accomplish in your life.
- **Build a Goal Worksheet:** Break down each master goal into smaller goals so you have tangible action steps or milestones you have to achieve in the next ninety days as you work toward achieving that master goal. It also has a progress tracker.
- **Conduct a Monthly, Weekly, and Daily Review:** Plan and prioritize your goals for the month, week, and day. The daily section includes an area for gratitude and positive affirmations as well as a daily schedule.

Since ambiguity is the enemy of accomplishment, the planner outlines how to set goals using the S.M.A.R.T.

(Specific, Measurable, Achievable, Relevant, and Time-Bound) goal-setting process.

What gives me joy and fulfillment are some of the great reviews we get from our customers. Here is my favorite:

"I have tried a host of planners over the years, and this has become my favorite. Life is a series of projects and this has such a practical method. Buy it!"

—TOM A.

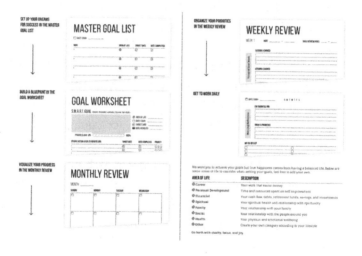

Figure 4.1[14]

---

14   ThisIsMyEra LLC, *#ThisIsMyEra 90-Day Planner* (Florida: ThisIsMyEra LLC, 2017), 4–5.

If you do not have a planning process in place, I would highly encourage you to try my planner. (You can get one at *www. SPEARMethod.com/resources.*)

In addition to the planner, I also offer an online academy through which you can take courses by subject-matter experts to help you with certain areas you want to learn more about. For instance, if personal financial planning is an area you struggle with, we have a course by an expert for that topic. This way, you have a guide who can help you in your journey in that area of life. However, feel free to explore other systems out there as well. The ultimate goal is for you to find a planning system that helps you get started on your planning journey and keeps you planning.

Now that you have a planning process you can implement, how do you know the right action steps to take to lead you to success? The answer is just a page turn away.

CHAPTER 5

A GOAL WITHOUT A PLAN IS JUST A WISH

———

It takes as much energy to wish as it does to plan.
—ELEANOR ROOSEVELT

Are champions born or made?
Is there a recipe for becoming a champion?

To me, a champion is someone who defeats and overcomes obstacles in their journey to achieve what they set out to do in life. I have always been fascinated by stories of people who have become champions in their own right: self-made millionaires (and billionaires) who started out poor but were able to overcome unimaginable obstacles to achieve success, professional athletes who grew up in the projects and denied the temptation of the path of least resistance and chose a life of sports versus selling drugs, artists and change agents who did not give up on their dreams and went on to beat the odds and became victors. To achieve such feats when the odds are stacked against you requires tenacity coupled with great planning.

But how feasible is becoming a champion? Take a professional basketball player as an example. According to the NCAA, out of more than half a million male high school basketball players each year, only 3.5 percent get to move on to play at the collegiate level.[15] Of those collegiate-level athletes, only 1.2 percent get to become professional players in the NBA.[16] Based on those statistics, only 0.01 percent of men's high school basketball players actually get to make it to play in the NBA. Of that 0.01 percent who get lucky enough to play professionally, only a handful get to win an NBA championship—so becoming a champion is not easy, but it is certainly possible.

Estimated Probability of Competing in Professional Athletics

	High School Participants	NCAA Participants	Overall % HS to NCAA	Approx. # Draft Eligible	# NCAA Drafted	% NCAA to Major Pro	% HS to Major Pro
Men's Basketball	540,769	18,816	3.50%	4181	52	1.20%	0.01%

Source: National Collegiate Athletic Association (NCAA)

---

15 "Estimated Probability of Competing in College Athletics," National Collegiate Athletic Association, accessed January 3, 2020.

16 "Estimated Probability of Competing in Professional Athletics," National Collegiate Athletic Association, accessed January 3, 2020.

Given the slim chance of making it to the NBA and eventually becoming an NBA champion, imagine the odds of winning it three times. That's what James "Champ" Jones did, and I was fortunate enough to interview him. This three-time NBA champion with the Miami Heat and Cleveland Cavaliers appeared on the #ThisIsMyEra podcast (launched after the planner). Although James Jones may not be as famous as the likes of former teammates Lebron James and Dwayne Wade, he is well respected. In fact, Lebron James said James Jones is his favorite player of all time and the greatest teammate he has ever had.[17]

To achieve all this success, James had to overcome many obstacles. He grew up in Carol City, Florida, a city not known for its NBA draft picks and where young people can easily find themselves involved in drugs and criminal activity. His mother was a teenager when James was born. Although she was a straight-A student, she sacrificed her college career so she could work and raise him.

With all the challenges that come with growing up in an inner city, James Jones was very much determined to crack the code of becoming a professional basketball player. Even though the odds were stacked against him, he was willing to do whatever it took to achieve his dream. He knew, however, the only way to make his dream come true was to develop a plan on how he was going to get there. As a curious child, James took time to seek his why, and once he found that

---

17 Dave McMenamin, "For the Cavaliers, There's a King and There's a Champ," *ESPN*, December 15, 2015.

his why was to become a professional basketball player, he started building his plan by asking questions like:

What does it take to be a professional basketball player?
What does that player look like?
What are the skill sets that player must possess?

By asking questions and searching for the answers, James Jones started learning what becoming a professional athlete entailed. They say success leaves clues, so the process he used to get answers to his questions was studying successful professional basketball players closely. Through this process of reverse engineering, he got a clear understanding of what they had done to be successful. With this insight, he was able to put together a plan for how he would go from playing in the inner-city neighborhood courts all the way to the NBA. Having a plan in place guided him on a totally different path than that of many of his inner-city peers who did not have a plan, per se, and just approached life as it came to them.

Having gone to college in South Florida, I can attest to the temptation of driving down to South Beach in Miami to have a good time. But not if you are James Jones. While at the University of Miami, when his teammates would go out on a Friday night to have fun, he would take the time to go to the gym and work on his craft. For him, "fun was becoming better and taking steps closer towards his dream." You will realize that at times your plan will require you to make short-term sacrifices in order to reap long-term rewards. Being disciplined enough to follow through is key to success.

What I have learned over time is that planning is not an event, something you do once and then are done with for the rest of your life. It is a process you engage in regularly as you discover new insights and achieve the milestones you had set out to do. Once he made it to the NBA, James did not stop planning for what is next. Knowing that the day would come when he would have to hang his boots, he repeated the same reverse-engineering planning process to make the transition from the court to the boardroom.

On July 19, 2017, after fourteen seasons in the NBA and winning three NBA championships, he was named vice president of basketball operations for the Phoenix Suns. On April 11, 2019, the team promoted him to the general manager role. Seeing what James Jones has accomplished, I am encouraged knowing that, if you are willing to take the time to ask the right questions and study others who have walked the road you want to walk, you can develop the blueprint for your dreams. All you need to do is apply action and make necessary adjustments along the way.

REVERSE ENGINEERING SUCCESS

When you have big dreams, you can easily get overwhelmed while trying to develop a plan on how to achieve that goal. If the dream is something anyone in your immediate network has never done, it can seem out of reach. That certainly was the case with me. Clearly, my chance meeting with Sara and learning her family's story (as you may recall from Chapter 2) changed my life. Through that experience, I developed a deep desire to empower others and positively impact those in need. Just like James Jones, I started studying people who were empowering others in a massive way. Through this process of reverse engineering, I was able to create a blueprint for how I would achieve my life's purpose.

One of the people I studied was Strive Masiyiwa, founder of Econet Global. I started following him in 1994, when I was still in primary school, around fourth grade. At that time, Strive had taken the Zimbabwe government to court for refusing to give his company, Econet Wireless, a license to operate Zimbabwe's first privately owned GSM cellular network license. This issue prompted a landmark constitutional case because going against then-Zimbabwe President Robert Mugabe's government was something not many Zimbabweans would consider doing, so his case attracted great public attention—a cause célèbre. Each day when my father came back from work, I would grab the newspaper from him to read any news articles on the case.

After five years, he won the landmark legal battle, which led to the removal of the state monopoly in telecommunications and opened the telecommunications sector to private competition. Today, Econet Wireless is now the leading provider of cellular service in Zimbabwe. In 1996, Strive and his wife launched a foundation to support orphaned and vulnerable children by primarily providing scholarship support and medical assistance.[18] To date, their foundation has provided over two hundred fifty thousand students with scholarships, invested over $60 million in health care and crisis response,

---

18 "About Us," Higher Life Foundation, accessed April 26, 2020.

and committed more than \$100 million to job creation through rural investments.[19]

Witnessing Strive's journey inspired me to follow in his footsteps. He left Zimbabwe and studied at the University of Wales.[20] My dream was to leave Zimbabwe after high school for an American education and then create a business that I would leverage to change lives across the world, starting with my home country. This goal may sound easy, but it is not a simple thing to accomplish when you are living a developing country. When I graduated high school in 2003, according to the World Bank, the annual average income (GDP per capita) in Zimbabwe was \$478, while the National Center for Education Statistics reported the average annual tuition cost at a US university was \$20,218.[21],[22] My parents had no way to possibly afford the cost of a four-year degree program—even if they had saved all their income for a lifetime. I needed to create a plan to get me there.

My plan was to work a summer job after graduating high school and use the earnings to pay for my SAT exams and also for membership at the US Educational Advising Center (USEAC), a center run by the US Embassy in Zimbabwe. The center provides comprehensive guidance to Zimbabwean students seeking to further their education in the United

19 "Home Page," Higher Life Foundation, accessed April 26, 2020.

20 Moky Makura, "Strive Masiyiwa—The Spiritual Entrepreneur," *Africa's Greatest Entrepreneurs*, (Cape Town: Penguin), 82–106.

21 "GDP per Capital (Current US\$)—Zimbabwe," The World Bank, accessed May 27, 2020.

22 "Tuition Costs of Colleges and Universities," National Center for Education Statistics, accessed March 12, 2020.

States.[23] As I look back now, these were probably the two most important investments I have ever made in my life.

My hope was that the center would help me develop a detailed action plan for identifying the appropriate universities for me and guiding me in completing the admissions and scholarship applications at these institutions.

I was not the only one in my class who harbored dreams of coming to the United States. I knew quite a number of classmates who also wanted to attend a US university. However, most of them were not willing to put in the time and effort to develop a plan. I am sure you can guess how their stories ended.

So back to my question: are champions born or made? In my opinion, champions are made. You may be born with natural talent, but if you do not nurture that talent carefully, you may never win the championship.

Becoming a champion starts with planning and ends with execution. Remember that success leaves clues, so take time to reverse engineer what your role models or other successful people have done to help you develop your plan.

Goals do not miraculously happen without action. That is why E, the next stage of the S.P.E.A.R method, is **execute**.

---

23 "Educational Advising," U.S. Embassy in Zimbabwe, accessed June 2, 2020.

PART THREE

EXECUTE

CHAPTER 6

DREAM BIG, START SMALL, ACT NOW

——

The only impossible journey is the one you never begin.
—TONY ROBBINS

Wayne Gretzky is one of the greatest ice hockey players to have ever played the sport. In fact, his nickname is "the Great One," mainly because of his many accomplishments during his twenty seasons in the NHL. At the time of this writing, Gretzky is the leading scorer in the NHL history and has won the Hart Memorial Trophy nine times as the most valuable player in the NHL.[24],[25] Although Gretzky was undoubtedly talented, talent alone could not have taken him to such great heights. The NHLer spent countless hours practicing: in his autobiography, he says, "From the age of three to the age of

---

24 "Skater Records—Most Goals, Career," National Hockey League, accessed April 13, 2020.

25 "NHL Hart Memorial Trophy Winners," National Hockey League, accessed April 13, 2020.

12, I could easily be out there for eight to 10 hours a day." You can get a sense of Gretzky's work ethic even from an early age.

Gretzky is not the only legend with a crazy work ethic. In the ten-part documentary *The Last Dance*, you can't help but notice that Michael Jordan's work ethic was one of the major reasons he reached the astronomical career heights with the all-conquering Chicago Bulls. In episode four of the documentary, after losing a playoff series to the Detroit Pistons, Jordan decided to spend that summer working out to better withstand the physical play of the Pistons. During that summer, Jordan added fifteen pounds of muscle and went on to win his first championship with the Bulls the next season, finally getting past the Pistons.[26] Another episode showed how Jordan spent the summer of 1995 filming *Space Jam* and training. He filmed Monday through Saturday from 7:00 a.m. to 7:00 p.m. with a two-hour break in between for working out and then had a basketball scrimmage with other NBA players from 7:00 p.m. to 10:00 p.m.[27] Jordan and the Bulls went on to win the season following this crazy busy summer. You see, to achieve great things, you must be willing to take action.

Any meaningful goal you set will not be achieved if you don't take action. No matter how much time you take seeking your why and detailing your plan, you will not achieve your goal without taking action. According to Gretzky, "You miss

---

26 Scott Davis, "Michael Jordan Once Added 15 Pounds of Muscle in One Summer To Prepare For A Rival And Changed The Way Athletes Train," *Insider.com*, April 27, 2020.

27 *The Last Dance*, episode 8, "Episode VIII," directed by Jason Hehir, featuring Michael Jordan, aired May 10, 2020, on ESPN.

100 percent of the shots that you do not take." If you never take the shot, you have no chance of achieving that goal or your life's purpose. That's why **execute** is the next step in the S.P.E.A.R. method after you complete your **plan**.

My friend and White House award-winning entrepreneur Felecia Hatcher illustrated the importance of taking action when I first saw her speaking. When she began her speech, she took out a $20 bill and asked the audience who wanted it. Almost everyone in the audience raised their hands, but no one took action to take the money. She asked again, and the same thing happened. On the third attempt, one lady had caught on to the lesson and rushed on stage and grabbed the money. By acting, this young lady became $20 richer, while the rest of the audience missed out on the money because of their inaction. Felecia then emphasized the lesson she had just demonstrated by saying, "Do not expect results for things that you did not work for."

Imagine the only way to feed your family is by hunting prey. You spend your days coming up with a plan on how to hunt deer. You even sharpen your spear. The day of the hunt, you head out early and spot a deer. It is in perfect sight, and all you need to do now is throw your spear for the kill. But you hesitate. You hesitate so long that something scares the deer and it runs off into the woods. Your inability to take action just cost you dinner. What will you tell your spouse and kids when you come back home emptyhanded from the hunt?

Once you take the time and effort to create a plan of attack, the rubber needs to meet the road. You need to take action and work the plan. Throw your spear so you can eat.

In the book *Execution*, authors Larry Bossidy and Ram Charan argue that execution, the ability to get things done, has become the sine qua non (absolutely necessary component) of management science. They point out that strategies most often fail because they are not executed well.

You may have heard the phrase, "Execution eats strategy for breakfast." It was coined by Jamie Dimon, CEO of JPMorgan Chase, and clearly outlines the importance of execution in your journey to success. Jamie would rather have a first-rate execution and second-rate strategy than a brilliant idea and mediocre execution.[28] No matter how well your strategy is planned out, if you do not take action, your beautiful strategy might as well have not existed in the first place.

That's why taking action and executing your plan is important. Through engaging with thousands of #ThisIsMyEra 90-day planner customers, I learned many people have difficulty getting started after they set a goal and develop an action plan. Since most goals require us to step outside our comfort zones, taking that first step can be challenging. Perhaps some of you may relate to this.

For three consecutive years, my wife, Ruth, listed running a 5K as one of her New Year's resolutions. The next day, she'd develop a twelve-month couch-to-race day plan. Then she'd shop for a few crucial running gear items—you need to look good while achieving your goal, right? A couple weeks later, her new running shoes would still be nicely packed in their

---

28 Rover Martin, "The Execution Trap," *Harvard Business Review*, (July/ August 2010).

box waiting to be worn. Around Valentine's Day, she'd run a mile here and a half-mile there but be well behind her running plan schedule. By St. Patrick's Day in mid-March, all her action would've ceased. Although she'd spent time developing a meticulous plan, her goal always got shelved until the next year.

Certainly, she is not the only one who has failed to execute a well-thought-out New Year's resolution plan. Millions of others, myself included, have done the same. A 2007 University of Bristol study showed that 88 percent of those who set New Year's resolutions fail.[29] Another study by the University of Scranton suggests that 92 percent of New Year's resolutions fail.[30] This problem is not just isolated to New Year's resolutions but to all goals, which begs the question: why do people fail to achieve their goals?

People fail to achieve their goals for many reasons. However, one that quickly comes to mind is not taking consistent action toward the achievement of the goal.

THE UNIVERSE REWARDS ACTION

After the third year of failing to achieve her goal of "running a 5K," Ruth and I tried a different approach. She needed to **seek** her why. Saying she wanted to run a 5K wasn't enough;

---

29   Jonah Lehrer, "Blame It on the Brain," *Wall Street Journal*, December 6, 2009

30   John C. Norcross, Marci S. Mrykalo, and Matthew D. Blagys, "Auld Lang Syne: Success Predictors, Change Processes, and Self-Reported Outcomes of New Year's Resolvers and Nonresolvers," *Journal of Clinical Psychology*, 58 (4) April 2002: 397–405.

she needed to know why she wanted to run a 5K. Upon reflection, Ruth realized she didn't feel like a runner. Even though she'd gone for short runs with her friends, she envied those who entered races. To her, those were the real runners. She knew that if she registered for and completed a 5K, she would truly feel like a runner. Given that she was stepping outside her comfort zone, she needed to connect deeply with her why.

Her **plan** had to center around registering for a race. That was the first step. She then worked backward from the day of the race to ensure she'd have enough training runs to race well.

Next, to **execute** her plan, we found a way to start small with a daily effort. James Clear, author of *New York Times* best-selling book *Atomic Habits,* provides a guide on how to form new habits that stick. A key pillar to forming a new habit is to start easy enough that you do not need motivation to do it. He says that rather than starting with fifty push-ups per day, you should start with five per day.[31] With this insight, Ruth began running two minutes and walking one minute every day for fifteen minutes total. Every week she added a little more run time and a little less walk time. By having the discipline to take consistent action daily, running became a new habit.

Three months later, she **achieved** her goal. She now has the medal and the satisfaction of knowing she is a 5K runner.

---

31   James Clear, "How to Build New Habits: This Is Your Strategy Guide," accessed March 6, 2020

The same thing happened to me. In 2014, I set the goal to write this book for the first time. When I created my book-writing plan, I scheduled four hours over the weekend to write. I reasoned that since I had work during the week, working in large chunks only on weekends would be easier. The strategy made sense on paper, but it was counterproductive in forming a new habit. With writing not in my comfort zone, not taking action daily on this goal made it difficult for me to engage over the weekend. Some weekends I would put in a solid couple of hours of work and then others I wouldn't. This inconsistency made me fail miserably, and after a couple months I gave up.

Four years later, I finally decided enough was enough. I followed the same process my wife used when she started running. First, I found a publishing company, New Degree Press (NDP), that was interested in publishing the book. Then I worked with the team at NDP to create my writing plan. They recommended I commit to writing for at least thirty minutes every day. Finding thirty minutes each day on an already packed scheduled is not easy, considering I run multiple businesses and a nonprofit, plus I have to make time for my family, working out, eating, and let's not forget sleeping. But, as they say, where there is a will, there is a way. I made sure that no matter what, I took action and wrote for at least thirty minutes each day. That would mean sometimes writing on the train while commuting to the office, working on the book during lunch, or waking up a little early to get those words in. By being disciplined enough to consistently write for at least thirty minutes each day, I was able to improve my writing and form a new habit. You are now reading the fruits of the consistent action I took in writing this book.

What seemed to be an "impossible" dream became possible. Remember that taking action is the thrust you give your spear as you launch it. The more consistent action you take, the more velocity (and force) your spear has, meaning it will arrive at the target sooner with more force.

THE EIGHTH WONDER OF THE WORLD

Albert Einstein once described compound interest as the eighth wonder of the world and the greatest power in the universe. When you think about his words, he's right. Let me first explain what compound interest is and then we can discuss how it applies to taking action.

I remember my high school teacher explaining what makes compound interest so powerful. To illustrate this point, I will compare compound interest to simple interest. Simple interest is based only on the principal amount of a loan or deposit, while compound interest is based on both the principal amount and the interest that accumulates on it in every period.

Let's say you deposit $10,000 into an investment account with 10 percent interest per year for a ten-year period—see the chart below to see how much you will have after ten years.

Compound Interest vs. Simple Interest

	Compound Interest	Simple Interest
Principal	$10,000	$10,000
Year 1	$11,000	$11,000
Year 2	$12,100	$12,000
Year 3	$13,310	$13,000
Year 4	$14,641	$14,000
Year 5	$16,105	$15,000
Year 6	$17,716	$16,000
Year 7	$19,487	$17,000
Year 8	$21,436	$18,000
Year 9	$23,579	$19,000
Year 10	$25,937	$20,000

As you can see, although we started with the same principal amount, using compound interest you earn almost $6,000 more in interest when compared to simple interest. Compound interest delivers exponential growth, which is more powerful than linear growth—do you see why it is the eighth wonder of the world?

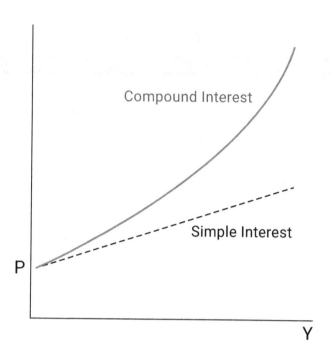

Figure 6.1

Now, this principle applies when taking action and executing steps toward the achievement of your goals. When you act consistently in pursuit of your goal, even with small action steps, you will achieve that goal much sooner because the frequent action you take will have a compounded effect on your actions. Think about the snowball effect, when something starts small and builds upon itself, becoming larger and larger over time. That's what will happen when you take consistent action toward a goal. In the beginning, you may see very minor results, but if you continuously take action, over time you will experience a great reward.

An example—let's say your goal is to lose fifty pounds in ninety days. If you take action toward that goal by exercising and eating healthy every day for ninety days, you will certainly increase your chances of achieving that goal more than if you were to work out and eat healthy once in a while, say every thirty days. By taking actions consistently, you will be able to benefit from the compounding effect of these actions and experience great gains over time.

At times, our goals may seem as big as a whale. How do you eat a whale? One bite at a time! So, I know at times when we set a BHAG (big hairy audacious goal), just the mere thought of the goal may paralyze us from taking action because of the big gulf separating where you are today from where you want to reach. If you fixate your focus on the end result, the process can get daunting. Instead, become obsessed with the next few steps you need to take, and before you know it, you will get to your goal.

Once you have set a goal and created your plan, you need to find a way to quickly take that first bite. The first bite can be a small one; what's important is taking the bite. Once you start, keep going. You want to be disciplined enough to consistently take action until the goal is achieved. If you are inconsistent in your execution, you will have difficulty getting into a rhythm that will help build up the snowballing effect momentum you need to achieve your goal. So, if your goal is to save money for your dream house, have a system in place where the money is automatically sent to your savings each month. If you are trying to get in shape, take up daily healthy habits that will get you where you need to be. The key is taking action consistently until you achieve your goal.

Feel free to dream big and start small, but always remember to act now.

The one obstacle that can prevent us from taking that first bite is fear. In the next chapter, I will share some tips for how to overcome your fears.

CHAPTER 7

FEAR IS THE ENEMY
OF SUCCESS

Fear is only as deep as the mind allows.

—JAPANESE PROVERB

We all have experienced fear in our lives—fear of failure, fear of rejection, fear of the unknown. Like it or not, who you are today and what you have been able to achieve thus far has, at one point, been influenced by fear. It is a powerful human emotion that we cannot escape. Like most things in life, fear is a two-sided coin. On one side, fear can be your friend. Biologically, fear can keep you safe by acting as an internal danger alarm. Our human brain is primarily wired for survival. When our brain's survival center perceives potential danger, the amygdala immediately turns on the switch for the fight/flight/freeze response mechanism. Without fear, some of us would not have lived as long as we have. But thanks to fear, we were able to trigger the fight/flight/freeze response mechanism that potentially saved our lives.

I recently experienced this response mechanism when my wife and I encountered a bear during a morning run in suburban New Jersey. What was an enjoyable running experience suddenly turned into panic when we saw the bear strolling down the street. We both froze and stopped running. Although we extremely worried that the worst was about to happen, we remained calm, not wanting to trigger a fight response mechanism in the bear. This incident happened at around 5:00 a.m., so no one was out at that time. It was just us and the bear. Luckily, a car drove down the street, scaring the bear away, and we were able to run back to our car.

The other side of the fear coin is not as good. If you allow it to, fear has the power to kill your ambitions and dreams. Fear can stop you from taking action, sabotaging your success. It can lead to self-doubt and keep you in your comfort zone. Fear can prevent you from fully experiencing life. As writer Suzy Kassem said, "Fear kills more dreams than failure ever will." Les Brown shared a similar sentiment when he said, "The graveyard is the richest place on earth, because it is here that you will find all the hopes and dreams that were never fulfilled . . . all because someone was **too afraid** to take that first step."

The reality is, if you allow it, fear can paralyze you, preventing you from taking that first step. Now, given that many of life's successes require you to take a risk, learning how to overcome fear is important. Fear will always exist, but you can learn how to not let fear hold you back. So instead of avoiding it, strive to conquer it. I still get the jitters right before I get on stage to give a speech—and this is coming from someone who has delivered keynote addresses in front of large audiences and in prestigious places like the United Nations. I have a routine I go through right before I get on stage that helps me overcome my fear and gets me in the right mental state. Learning to control and overcome your fears is a key life skill to master if you want to execute your life plan at the highest level. In fact, mastering this skill can take your life from ordinary to extraordinary.

In the last chapter, we discussed the importance of taking consistent action toward achieving your goals. When you dissect the cells of every success story, you will find that action-taking is at their nucleus. In fact, when it comes to your goals and life's purpose, not acting out of fear is a bigger failure than faltering after an attempt to achieve the goal.

MINDSET IS EVERYTHING

At Camp Mavericks 2019 in Pocono Springs, Pennsylvania, my life was profoundly changed. I confronted and overcame one of my biggest fears: the fear of failure. I found out about the Maverick community, an exclusive global network of leading entrepreneurs, while reading a book called *Never Lose a Customer Again* by Joey Coleman. Through a series of unbelievable events, a couple weeks after finding out about this community, I was invited to one of their events—Camp Maverick. Simply put, Camp Maverick is a camp for adults. You get to spend a few days in the woods with a group of exceptional entrepreneurs and to disconnect from the world but connect as a group and with yourself. As Camp Maverick likes to describe it, over the course of almost a week, "campers get to dare greatly, learn deeply, and make incredible connections that have the potential to last a lifetime."

Talk about daring greatly: one of the surprise exercises they had lined up one evening was a fire walk. A fire walking exercise is designed to help you learn how to conquer fear and show you what is possible as you unleash the power within yourself. It is a great tool to help you break through limiting beliefs. When they told us about it, I was fully convinced I would not do it. Although getting burned was a legitimate concern, that was not what was stopping me from wanting to do the fire walk. What stood in my way was the fear that I would fail in front of everyone. I was totally comfortable watching others do it because the thought of walking across a bed of 1,200°F hot coals was not something on my bucket list. Watching the event staff prepare the hot coals and feeling the heat of the coals from a distance also amplified my fear.

Even as other campers started walking across the hot coals, bellowing loud, victorious screams at the end, I still could not get myself to do it. I did not want to be that guy who failed while everyone else walked across successfully. Fear of failure can prevent us from moving forward in life and make us miss out on great opportunities.

As I watched more and more campers walk on fire, I realized I was allowing fear to rob me of an amazing personal growth experience. In fact, I was being hypocritical and not in alignment with one of the core messages I give during my speeches. I always evangelize that to grow, we need to step outside of our comfort zones. I also always share the importance of embracing the N.O.W.—No Opportunity

Wasted. The N.O.W. concept started when I was thinking about launching the Amani Hope Foundation. Part of me wanted to wait until I was more established before launching the foundation. I realized, however, that I would be wasting the opportunity to make an impact today, so I decided to launch the foundation, and N.O.W. became my mantra. Why wait to do something tomorrow that you can do today? Here I was, presented with a perfect opportunity to step outside my comfort zone and also overcome a fear, but I was allowing fear to hold me back and keep me rooted in my comfort zone. Thinking about this reality did not sit well with me. I was deeply conflicted.

With a few people left to go, I knew the time was now or never. I took a deep breath and decided to make that leap of faith and joined the queue. I decided to follow John Maxwell's advice of "feeding your faith and starving your fears." I felt as if I had just accepted an altar call at church as I took steps toward the burning coals. As the line moved forward, my heart pounded harder and harder. I remember at one point having a vision of myself getting burned, but I immediately took that thought captive and replaced it with one of me celebrating conquering the challenge.

Realizing I had the power to assign whatever meaning I wanted to the term "failure," I decided to define an unsuccessful attempt to fire walk as a learning experience. I also remembered the sheer number of risks an average person takes every day without even thinking about it or feeling an ounce of fear. For example, each time you drive, you are taking a risk and face a chance of failing to make it back home. But people take that risk all the time without a second thought. According to the 2018 "Global Status Report on Road Safety" by the World Health Organization (WHO), at least 1.35 million road traffic deaths occur every year. That means someone dies on the road every twenty-four seconds.[32]

Before you know it, my turn to walk over the coals arrived—the moment of truth. I knew the moment I set foot on the coals that I just had to keep walking forward to prevent being burned. Once I started taking action, I had to consistently do so until I reached the end of the bed of coals. I took a deep breath in, made that first step, and kept walking at my normal pace until the end. When I made it across the bed of hot coals, I felt a rush of joyful emotions erupt in me. I had done it. I had just walked on fire and came out of it with no burns. Like the other campers, I let out a powerful roar as soon as I realized I had done it. I had conquered my fear and done something I never thought I was able to do.

That fire walking experience taught me that mindset is everything when it comes to taking action and achieving your greatest potential. Mindset is defined as a mental attitude. The word itself is a combination of two words, "mind" and "set"—so I like to think of it as having your mind inclined in a certain direction.

When faced with challenges, our mental attitude toward fear can be the determining factor in whether we act or not. Basically, our mindsets play an important role in how we each deal with challenges. When I was faced with the challenge

---

32 "Global Status Report on Road Safety 2018," World Health Organization, accessed February 16, 2020.

of walking on fire, I had to shift my mindset in order to take action. Instead of running away from the challenge of fire walking, I decided to confront it head-on by activating my "champion mindset" (some like to call it a "warrior mindset").

In Chapter 5, we discussed a champion being someone who defeats and overcomes obstacles in their journey to achieve what they set out to do in life. We can all turn that champion mindset switch on in the midst of fear. The key is to acknowledge the presence of the obstacle without focusing on it. What you should focus on is the outcome you want to achieve and the actions you are going to take to achieve this outcome. A great golfer acknowledges the hazards on the course, such as trees, sandpits, and lakes, but they focus their attention on the outcome—the trajectory they want the ball to take when they drive it toward the hole.

CONSCIOUS RISK-TAKING

Let's face it: doing hard things can be scary. The path of least resistance is always the most tempting in any given situation. Sometimes it is the smart thing to do, but in some cases, taking this path is just sheer laziness. By always taking the easy route, we run the risk of training our minds to always stay in our comfort zone.

Comfort zones are those safe spaces where our behaviors fit a pattern that minimizes stress and risk. A comfort zone provides a sense of familiarity, mental security, and certainty. It is that happy place where the brain releases feel-good chemicals—dopamine and serotonin. Our brain actually loves to be in that comfortable place because it gets to be on autopilot. In other words, your brain wants to lounge around in a metaphorical hammock on a warm summer day. The problem with staying in your comfort zone is that doing so inhibits your personal growth. As Tony Robbins likes to say, "If you are not growing, you are dying." You must constantly do things that lead to growth, and you can only experience growth when you take risks and step outside your comfort zone

Similar to how you can train a muscle to become stronger through exercise, you can train your mind to have stronger mental strength by doing things outside your comfort zone. So, basically, you can train your mind to have the champion mindset by consciously facing and overcoming our fears. As you build this muscle, you will experience growth in your ability to overcome the temptation to procrastinate or avoid taking the difficult, yet necessary, actions to achieve your goals.

In her book *Art of the Risk*, Kayt Sukel says taking risks is necessary. "It's such an integral component to learning and growth. It's really important for people to start integrating more small risks and building up from there in their lives—not just from a learning perspective, but from a joy and enjoyment perspective too."[33]

One effective way I found that trains you to activate your champion mindset is through what I call conscious risk-taking: when you make the choice to go against the will of your

---

33 Katie Rose Quandt, "Who Gets to Be a Risk Taker?" *Headspace* (blog), accessed March 6, 2020.

brain to do something uncomfortable. Now, I am not talking about doing something stupid, like driving on the highway at one hundred fifty miles per hour—in fact, certain risks are not worth taking. I am talking about doing something hard each day that gets you out of your comfort zone. You can do something as simple as taking a cold shower or doing a hard workout you have never done before.

Former Navy SEAL David Goggins has mastered the power of his mind through conscious risk-taking. In his book, *Can't Hurt Me: Master Your Mind and Defy the Odds*, David shares his astonishing life story and reveals that most of us tap into only 40 percent of our capabilities. David calls this the 40 percent rule. His life story shows how anyone can demolish fear and reach their full potential. Seeking a career change from being an exterminator, David wanted to join the Navy SEALs. But he had one big problem—his weight. David had to lose 106 pounds in three months to hit the 191-pound weight limit to enlist as a Seal. This feat seemed nearly impossible, but David had a realization. "I first realized that not all physical and mental limitations are real, and that I had a habit of giving up way too soon," he wrote in his book.

David became convinced that your mind will tell you to give up when your body has only reached 40 percent of its potential. You see, one move past 40 percent effort and you are outside your comfort zone—a place your brain does not want to go. Yet you still have 60 percent of effort left in you. So, if we don't consciously train our minds to go the extra mile, we will always default to safety—to our comfort zone, the place where stress and risk are minimized. By constantly challenging himself, David has been able to achieve some great feats. In 2010, he ran a twenty-four-hour ultramarathon by himself while others ran as relay teams. He later broke a Guinness World Record by completing 4,030 pull-ups in seventeen hours. He is also believed to be the only member of the armed forces who is a NAVY SEAL and US Army ranger, and has completed Air Force tactical air controller training. Just completing one of these is a feat.

Do not let your own potential go to waste. Make a habit each day of conscious risk-taking. I recommend doing a hard task in the morning because you can then take on the rest of your day with that win already in your pocket. Having that positive mental reference will help you confront a challenge that requires you to step outside of your comfort zone in your quest to achieve your goal. The more comfortable you get with the uncomfortable, the more you can confront and overcome fears. The more fears you are able to overcome, the more you will be able to execute in your quest to achieve your goal.

Clearly, fear can be what's holding you back from your life's purpose. Taking conscious risks to help you overcome fears and become comfortable with the uncomfortable is worth doing. In the next chapter, I will cover how courage and discipline can be your best allies in your quest to surmount your fears.

CHAPTER 8

FORTUNE FAVORS THE BOLD

He who is not courageous enough to take risks will accomplish nothing in life.

—MUHAMMAD ALI

Sub-Saharan summers can get quite hot—as was the case on this day in Harare, Zimbabwe. So as soon as I heard the ice cream truck on my street, I raced down our driveway as fast as my nine-year-old legs could, barefoot and full-steam ahead. I knew when I got inside the house, I had no margin for error if I were to get an ice cream on that hot summer day. I had to find my mother as quickly as possible, make my ice cream request persuasively, get the money, and race back to the gate before the ice cream truck went past the Smiths' house. I never ventured past the Smiths' house. The house next to theirs had two large Rottweilers that always barked at people when they walked past. I was afraid the dogs would jump the fence and attack me, so as soon as the ice cream truck passed the Smiths' house, it was a lost cause.

"Mama, where are you?" I screamed loudly as soon as I got into the house.

She yelled back, "I'm here." From the sound of her voice, I knew she was in the sewing room, so I headed straight over. Gasping for air, I stated my request with confidence and a smile: "Can I please get some money for a Ninja Turtle ice cream?"

Without even looking back at me, my mom nonchalantly replied, "No," and continued with her sewing as if I were not even there.

Immediately I realized this interaction was not going to be the quick Formula 1 pit stop I had envisioned. I had to work for this one. I asked again, this time pulling on her hand, hoping the nagging would make her give in.

She looked at me straight in my eyes and said, "You were naughty this morning when we had guests over, so this week you'll not get any money from me for ice cream."

With the sound of the ice cream truck receding now, I knew the truck was way past the Smiths' house. Today was a lost cause. I felt helpless. I thought to myself, *Why does my mother have the power to decide my ice cream destiny?* I started searching for answers. I wanted to find a way to make sure such powerlessness would never happen to me again. I wanted to be in control of whether I had an ice cream or not.

As I sat on the lawn pondering, I noticed that my neighbor's windows were rather dirty. Looking back now, I realize this moment was one of the most impactful of my life. And it all started when an idea popped into my head. *What if I clean her windows and make some money for ice cream tomorrow?* In an instant, I got up, ran to the house, grabbed a bucket and my mother's cleaning supplies, and headed over to Mrs. Gutsa's house.

When I arrived, I hesitated to knock on her door as thoughts of self-doubt started swirling in my head. *I have never cleaned windows before. What if I am not good at it?* After a little back-and-forth internal debate, I decided I really had nothing to lose. Plus, I really wanted to have ice cream money for tomorrow, and I knew if I didn't proceed, I would be back at my mother's mercy. So, I knocked.

When she answered, I pitched my window-cleaning service. Mrs. Gutsa was poker-faced the entire time, so I wasn't sure if she liked what she was hearing or if I was wasting her time. An awkward silence ensued after my sales pitch. Right before I was about to thank her for her time and head back home in defeat, she asked, "Will you be done by sunset? And how much is it?" Those words were music to my ears, and I replied, "Today's special deal is ZWD$5 and yes, I will be done by sunset." We shook hands, and with that, I started my first business at nine years old.

Since I had never washed a window before in my life, this task was unfamiliar territory and certainly not in my comfort zone. In my mind, I thought the job would be easy—I mean, how hard could it be to wash windows? I had estimated doing the entire house would only take about thirty minutes. Boy, was I wrong. An hour into the project, I was not even halfway done, and I started asking myself, *What were you thinking?*

I considered quitting a few times. All I wanted to do was go home, lay on the couch, and watch cartoons—like my friends. That was certainly my comfort zone. But I knew if I didn't follow through, my situation would never change. So, I had to exercise a generous amount of self-discipline and kept pushing forward. Three painful hours later, I earned my first ZWD$5 in business. Fortune truly favors the bold.

The next day, when the ice cream truck came by, I bought that Ninja Turtle ice cream with my own money. No more asking Mum. In one day, by stepping outside my comfort zone and into the "growth zone," I experienced growth. Cleaning windows for three hours on a hot summer day was not easy, but I pushed through the pain and didn't quit. I knew the pain was temporary. I also knew the pain I would experience if I had quit would last longer and be way more painful.

If I had not been bold enough to take action, I wouldn't have started my first business and enjoyed a summer filled with ice cream. In the words of Paul J. Meyer, "Success requires action. Before you can have, you just do." The key tenet of the **execute** stage in the S.P.E.A.R. method is taking action, because without taking any action, you will not move toward your desired outcome. But let's face it: taking action is not always easy at times, because it may mean stepping outside your comfort zone and doing things you have never done before.

3 LIFE ZONES

Over time, I have grown to learn that life consists of three zones we can choose to live in at any given time: the "comfort zone," the "growth zone," and the "dangerous zone." As we have discussed earlier, your comfort zone is a psychological state in which you feel safe or at ease and without stress or anxiety. The danger of staying in your comfort zone is that it hinders your personal growth, since you are not being challenging to do things out of what you consider normal.

For example, how much growth will you experience if you were to do the same routine every day? Let's say you did the same workout daily—you run two miles on the treadmill at the same pace five days a week for an entire year. You would be in your comfort zone, but you would not experience any growth.

To improve, you must move out of your comfort zone into the "growth zone." This zone is where miracles happen, since you push yourself beyond your comfort levels. Using the earlier example, instead of doing the same two miles at the same pace, you want to change things up by increasing your pace and your distance over time. This way, you can improve your endurance and your speed and experience growth. You will experience some pain in the growth zone, but this is an indicator of learning and growth.

Then you have the "dangerous zone": the zone your mother warned you about. You do not want to be in this zone because it may lead to severe consequences. The dangerous zone is where you attempt things that are damaging and even life-threatening—for instance, climbing Mount Everest without proper training. Nick Sednew knows what being in the dangerous zone feels like. In 2009, while he was working aboard a cruise ship sailing between Antarctica and the southern tip of South America, the ship was hit by a powerful storm.[34] The ship's captain told everyone to stay inside, and warning signs blocked the doors to the decks, but Sednew did not heed the warnings and went out on the deck. He wanted to experience the full force of an Antarctic storm.

The heavy rain and wind were so strong that when he tried to run back inside, he fell and broke his nose and cut his lip. By clinging to the railings, Sednew was able to prevent himself from being blown overboard. He is lucky to have survived that ordeal and get to tell the story.

Many people feel the same urge Sednew felt—the desire to venture past the limits of safety in pursuit of a rewarding experience. However, such risky desires can be deadly, so you should proceed with caution when you are considering doing something past the growth zone.

---

34 Natalie Wolchover, "Why Do People Take Risks?" *Live Science*, August 30, 2011.

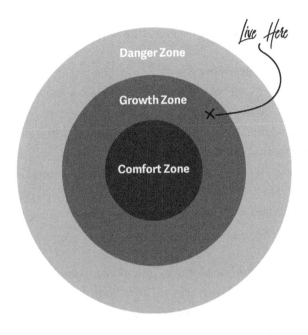

Figure 8.1

SELF-DISCIPLINE AND COURAGE

Self-discipline and courage are the fuel for your execution vehicle that will take your plan forward by overcoming the temptation to stay in your comfort zone. Self-discipline is the ability to pursue what you think is right despite temptations to abandon it.[35] It is the management of yourself for the sake of improvement.[36] According to a report from a meta-analysis study (examination of data from a number of independent studies of the same subject in order to determine overall

---

35   Lexico, s.v. "self-discipline (_n._)," accessed May 6, 2020

36   Merriam-Webster, s.v. "self-discipline (_n._)," accessed May 9, 2020

trends), a high level of self-discipline facilitates success, better accomplishments, and achievement of goals.[37]

Unfortunately, many people admit that self-discipline is a trait they do not have. A survey conducted by the American Psychological Association shows that 27 percent of adults in the United States do not have enough self-discipline to improve their life and make necessary changes.[38] Given this statistic, developing self-discipline is like having a super-power. Since self-discipline is a learned behavior, it requires practice and repetition to integrate it into your day-to-day life.

Best-selling author Jennifer Cohen recommends removing temptations and distractions from your environment as a crucial first step when working to improve your self-discipline.[39] For instance, if you are trying to eat better, get rid of all the junk food in your house so you are not easily tempted. If you want to improve your focus and productivity, turn off your cell phone and remove clutter from your working area. In his book *The Miracle Morning*, Hal Elrod recommends placing the alarm out of your arm's reach so you actually have to leave your bed to turn it off and avoid the temptation

37   Denise T.D. de Ridder, G. Lensvelt-Mulders, C. Finkenauer, M.F. Stock, and R.F. Baumeister, "Taking Stock of Self-Control: A Meta-Analysis of How Trait Self-Control Relates to a Wide Range of Behaviors," *Personality and Social Psychology Review* 16, 1 (February 2012): 76–99.

38   "Stress in America: Our Health at Risk," American Psychological Association, retrieved March 12, 2020.

39   Jennifer Cohen, "5 Proven Methods for Gaining Self Discipline," *Forbes*, June 18, 2014.

of just hitting the snooze button if you are trying to be more disciplined with waking up early.[40]

Developing self-discipline can be painful process. But if you do not build it, the regret you will experience as a result of not being self-disciplined hurts more—so enduring the pain of discipline now is better than the pain of regret later. Jim Rohn said, "We must all suffer from one of two pains: the pain of discipline or the pain of regret. The difference is discipline weighs ounces while regret weighs tons." To face the pain of self-discipline, you must have courage.

The Merriam-Webster dictionary defines courage as the "mental or moral strength to venture, persevere, and withstand danger, fear, or difficulty."[41] Stepping out of your comfort zone into the growth zone as you execute toward the achievement of your goals will require you to tap into your courage bank now and again. Being courageous doesn't mean you're not afraid. It means you don't let fear stop you from taking action.

Kerri Strug's story at the 1996 Summer Olympics in Atlanta, Georgia, is one that illustrates true courage. With the Russians dominating the Olympic women's gymnastics event since 1948, no US women's gymnastics team had ever taken Olympic gold. In the Olympic finals against the Russians and with the Americans enjoying a commanding lead, things started to take an unexpected turn. The first four American vaulters did not have great landings, and Dominique

---

40 Hal Elrod, The Miracle Morning, (Hal Elrod International Inc., 2016), 44–45.

41 Merriam-Webster, s.v. "courage (_n._)," accessed April 11, 2020.

Moceanu fell twice back-to-back, which severely cut the US lead.

Now the Russians were looking at another potential victory. Strug was up last for the Americans, and on her first vault, like Moceanu, she fell as well, and the awkward landing gave out a loud crack as two ligaments in her ankle were torn apart. The Americans now faced a dilemma. Since their lead had been severely cut, to guarantee a gold medal finish required Strug to go again. If she didn't, the Russians had a chance to close the margin and win the gold. Although she was in pain, Strug made the courageous decision to go one more time. She ran the seventy-five feet before executing her vault, landing on her hurt ankle, and holding her pose long enough for the judges to recognize her before collapsing on the ground in pain. Her score for that run was 9.712—enough to guarantee the US women their first Olympic gold medal and end the Russian domination.[42]

Undoubtedly, Strug's courageous decision could have resulted in a serious, life-changing injury. No one would have faulted her for not risking it. But she was courageous enough to do it and now has a gold medal to show for it. Imagine the painful feeling of regret Kerri Strug would have carried all her life if she had made the decision not to take action and do that final run. That feeling of regret would have certainly weighed tons and lasted a lifetime. It would have certainly been more painful when compared to the temporary pain she suffered in that last run.

---

42 Mike Penner, "U.S. Gymnast Braves Pain for Gold," *LA Times*, July 24, 1996.

To some degree the same is true for me, although not as an Olympic athlete but rather a window-cleaning entrepreneur. When I was cleaning windows, the experience was not pleasant, and I was so close to quitting. The other kids my age were having fun playing or watching TV while I spent hours cleaning dirty windows in the hot summer sun. The work was physically demanding. However, that pain was short-lived, and the benefits from that pain not only provided the gratification through a generous supply of ice creams, but also a lifelong lesson that has shaped my decision-making process ever since.

THE MOST IMPORTANT CONVERSATION

As you work toward achieving your goals, you will be confronted with situations that will require you to develop self-discipline and courage. Mastering self-talk is essential. Self-talk is probably the most important conversation we have regularly. In the moments before Kerri Strug did that last run, imagine the conversation going on in her mind. I do believe the words she said to herself in that moment gave her the courage to do that last run.

Take each thought captive and think through what you say to yourself. Is your self-talk empowering or disempowering? Self-talk is a form of neuro-linguistic programming (NLP) and possesses significant power over our minds and ultimately our behaviors. Since self-talk can be both positive and negative, you want your internal conversations to be positive self-talk. A good way to develop a positive self-talk habit is by scheduling time to say positive affirmations to yourself.

In the chapter, I will share how I have incorporated positive affirmation statements in my daily routine.

Public speaker and best-selling author Robert Richman described how subtle language changes influence how our brains perceive different situations. He shared how making subtle shifts in your language can make a huge difference in how your brain perceives the information. For example, shifting from "I am tired" to "I feel tired" can make a huge difference, because "I am" statements are identifying statements. You want to make sure your brain associates your identity with something that empowers and uplifts you rather than something that attacks your self-confidence.[43]

I fully agree with Henry Ford when he said, "Whether you think you can, or you think you can't—you're right." So make sure whatever you believe and subsequently tell yourself aligns with your goals. As individuals, we have limitless potential, but what will determine whether we reach that potential or not is really centered on our willingness and desire to get out of the comfort zone. Are you willing to be bold enough to take the necessary action to achieve your potential? Growth truly comes by doing things you have not done before, which requires courage to move forward in the face of fear. Having the self-discipline to continuously do what needs to be done to become successful is key. Forming winning habits will catalyze your efforts and make the **execute** stage a breeze.

---

43   Cheyenne Diaz, "The Staggering Power of Self Talk on the Body and Mind," *MindValley* (blog), January 23, 2018.

CHAPTER 9

HABITS SHAPE YOUR DESTINY

———

We are what we repeatedly do. Excellence, then, is not an act, but a habit.

—ARISTOTLE

What is the first thing you do when you wake up every morning?

Do you meditate, pray, or spend some time in silence?

Do you hit the snooze button a few times before you finally wake up and realize you're going to be late (again)?

Do you exercise? Or smoke a cigarette?

Our daily rituals and habits shape our current and future realities. Good daily rituals and habits are like oxygen for success. Bad rituals and habits will suffocate your success.

According to cognitive neuroscientists, up to 95 percent of our daily actions are rituals and habits performed on auto-pilot.[44] Take a moment and let that sink in—only 5 percent of our actions are conscious. Therefore, making the conscious decision to improve your daily rituals and habits will increase your chances of executing at your highest potential and achieving success.

Here is a way I like to look at it: imagine two teenage clones, genetically identical in their biological makeup; everything about them is the same. The clones have grown up together, going through the same life situations every second of their existence. Both clones view success the same way and **both want to achieve the same goals in life**. The only difference between the two clones are their daily rituals and habits as illustrated in the table below:

The Habits of Twin Clones

Clone A	Clone B
Wakes up early and does an empowering morning ritual.	Wakes up whenever, usually after snoozing the alarm clock a few times.
Gets at least eight hours of quality sleep each night.	Sleeping routine is erratic; some days only gets three hours of sleep.
Exercises for at least thirty minutes each day.	Does not have a consistent exercise schedule. Can go for weeks without exercising.
Spends time each morning reviewing goals and setting a plan for the day.	Does not have a routine to plan their day and review goals; just takes each day as it comes.
Reads for at least thirty minutes daily.	Lucky to read for thirty minutes in a month.

---

44 Marianne Szegedy-Maszak, "Mysteries of The Mind," Auburn University, accessed March 25, 2020.

Remember everything about them is the same from a biological and intelligence standpoint. They share the same life goals. The only difference is their daily habits. Based on what you know about the clones, which clone do you think stands a chance at achieving the goals they set? Unless the goal is to fail in life, Clone A stands the best chance of achieving their goals and becoming successful.

By researching the habits of 177 self-made millionaires, author Tom Corley explains in his best-selling book *Change Your Habits, Change Your Life* that successful individuals set themselves up to achieve by consistently following specific success habits. Examining the habits used by successful people and incorporating them into your daily routine will certainly help you achieve your goals. Let us jump into some of the habits successful people have.

THE MIRACLE MORNING

"If you win the morning, you win day."

My high school days attending boarding school laid the seeds for my daily morning routine. We were required to wake at 5:00 a.m. every day, and as a result I learned to be an early riser. I am usually up by 4:00 a.m. every day, weekends included. This habit is now hardwired in me, to the point when I even wake up around the same time every day without the help of an alarm clock. Waking up early allows me to quickly get started on the important tasks while my brain is alert and there are minimal distractions. With this time, I am extremely productive, and by the time 9:00 a.m. rolls around, I have usually knocked out a few high-priority tasks. My business partner, Alexander Star, used to find it fascinating that by the time he got up around 7:00 a.m., he would find his email inbox flooded with emails.

I am not the only early riser. Apple CEO Tim Cook has been quoted saying he rises at 3:45 a.m. PST, so he can get a little work in before his colleagues on EST. Oprah Winfrey said she wakes up around 6:00 a.m. to reflect, meditate, and exercise before going into the office. However, the prize most likely goes to Mark Wahlberg, who apparently wakes up at 2:30 a.m. to work out and start the day.[45]

Waking up early alone is not what will make you productive and successful. What you do after you wake up sets you up for success. When I was in college, I noticed the difference in the outcome of my day based on how I started the day. The days I woke up early and spent hours in bed on the phone scrolling through social media and doing nothing weren't productive days for me. I would find myself having low energy throughout the day and not really "feeling it." The days I would wake up and immediately get out of bed, go work out, take a shower, plan my day, and read before I started my day were when I experienced peak productivity. Looking to capitalize on this insight, I went on a quest to find the best morning routines that would help me become even more productive and achieve my goals.

In my search, I found Hal Elrod's book *The Miracle Morning: The Not-So-Obvious Secret Guaranteed to Transform Your Life (Before 8AM)*. With nearly 3,700 five-star Amazon reviews,

---

45 Bryan Lufkin, "Is waking up early good or bad?" *BBC*, February 13, 2019.

this book is certainly a crowd favorite, and I highly recommend it. This book is great if you are looking to establish daily rituals that will help you execute at your highest level. In the book, Hal shares the SAVERS model, a six-step morning routine he developed. SAVERS is an acronym that stands for Silence, Affirmation, Visualization, Exercise, Reading, and Scribing (writing/journaling).[46]

Hal's life has been anything but easy. At age twenty, he survived a life-threatening car accident that left him in a coma. At age thirty-seven, he overcame a rare and aggressive form of cancer (acute lymphoblastic leukemia). At one point in his life, he was bankrupt and had to start over again. Hal's SAVERS model helped him achieve success and harness his full potential, although he has had to deal with some tough cards in life. He has gone on to become an ultramarathoner, international keynote speaker, and author, all by age thirty. Hal also stated his book has transformed the lives of hundreds of thousands of people, helping them wake up each day "with more energy, focus, and motivation" to tackle their goals.[47]

Silence Affirmations Visualization Exercise Reading Scribing

Figure 9.1

---

46 Elrod, The Miracle Morning, 53–89.

47 Locke Hughes, "I tried the 'The Miracle Morning' productivity routine for a month. Here's what happened," *NBC News*, March 17, 2019.

After reading Hal's book, I decided to try the SAVERS model for a month to see what would happen. I was impressed by the results. Since my morning routine already included time for silence, exercise, and reading, adding affirmations, visualization, and scribing to the routine made it even more powerful.

My morning routine now follows an enhanced SAVERS approach. I typically wake up at 4:00 a.m., brush my teeth, go into my home office, pray, and study the Bible for the first thirty minutes (silence). Then, I get dressed and head to the gym (exercise). Before my workout, I do breathing exercises following the Wim Hof method—breathing techniques that were scientifically proven to improve your energy level, detox your body, reduce stress levels, rebalance the nervous system, and strengthen your immune system (to learn more, go to *www.wimhofmethod.com*).[48] After my workout, I take a hot and cold shower (alternating the temperature of the water from hot to cold water at least three times throughout the shower, ending with a cold shower—see next table for details). Research has shown that this type of shower has many health benefits, such as increasing blood circulation and improving detoxification, mood, and energy.[49] The hot and cold shower is my coffee. After the shower, I am fully awake and ready to take on the world.

---

48   "Benefits," Wim Hof Method, accessed January 14, 2020.

49   A. Mooventhan and L. Nivethitha, "Scientific Evidence-Based Effects of Hydrotherapy on Various Systems of the Body," *North American Journal of Medical Sciences* 6, 5 (May 2014): 199–209.

Hot & Cold Alternating Shower Directions

My Hot & Cold Shower Protocol:
1. Start with a three-minute regular shower in hot water.
2. Turn the dial to cold for thirty seconds (I like to go as cold as possible).
3. Switch back to hot for thirty seconds.
4. Repeat three times, ending with cold water.

I then spend forty-five minutes journaling, planning, and reviewing my goals in my #ThisIsMyEra 90-day planner (scribing & visualization). Once I am done with my goals, I read my affirmation statements aloud (affirmation). I am lifelong learner, so I love reading and learning new things; for my hourlong commute into Manhattan, I read a book or listen to a podcast (reading). Following this morning ritual helps me get centered and provides focus on what my top priorities are for the day. It also helps me start the day in a peak state full of energy, so as I execute on my goals, I have clarity and energy to push through. You need to establish a morning ritual that gets you ready for the day and executing at the highest possible level, none of which is possible without a good night's sleep.

SLEEP YOURSELF TO SUCCESS

I remember reading Sangu Delle's biography and asking myself, "Does this guy sleep?" You see, Sangu is the chairman of Golden Palm Investments Corporation (GPI), an investment holding company focused on building world-class technology companies in Africa. GPI has backed startups such as Andela (a tech company that has raised more than $100 million from investors, including Mark Zuckerberg), mPharma, and Flutterwave.[50] GPI portfolio companies have raised over $500 million in venture financing. Sangu is also the managing director of Africa Health Holdings, an innovative company based in West Africa, focused on building Africa's health care future. Sangu is also the cofounder of Cleanaway, a nonprofit working in underdeveloped communities in Ghana to make sure water, sanitation, and basic human rights are provided. The organization has been able to bring clean water and sanitation to over two hundred thousand people in 160 villages in Ghana.[51] Sangu is also an author and a speaker.

Born and raised in Ghana, Sangu made his way to Harvard University, where he graduated with highest honors in African studies and economics. As a postgraduate student, he was awarded the Soros Fellowship and pursued a JD at Harvard Law School and an MBA at Harvard Business School.

In 2016, he was a finalist for Young CEO of the Year by the Africa CEO Forum. He was also selected as a TEDGlobal Fellow and named among *Forbes*'s top thirty most promising entrepreneurs in Africa. Sangu has trekked Mount Everest and summited Mount Kilimanjaro. To date, he has read more than five thousand books, traveled to forty-seven of the fifty-four African countries, and interviewed more than six hundred African entrepreneurs along the way.[52] Clearly, Sangu is a busy man.

---

50   Kori Hole, "Andela's $700 Million Valuation Puts Africa's Tech Ecosystem at Risk," *Forbes*, October 3, 2019.

51   "Responsibility," Gold Palm Investments, accessed January 3, 2020.

52   Sangu Delle, "Home Page," accessed January 5, 2020.

When I chatted with Sangu, I was curious to find out his secrets for time management and productivity. How was he able to work on multiple projects at the same time and still deliver high-quality output? Sangu pointed out that quality sleep is a key ingredient in his winning productivity formula. However, this was not always the case for him. For more than twenty years of his life, Sangu used to take pride in the fact that he only slept an average of four hours a night. Sleep was not a priority for him, but this mindset changed after he read the book *Why We Sleep* by Matthew Walker and realized all the negative consequences that come with a lack of adequate sleep and how his sleeping habits were actually counterproductive. After reading the book, Sangu now prioritizes sleep and aims for at least eight hours of sleep each night.

In the book, Walker shares why sleep is one of the most important but least understood aspects of our life, wellness, and longevity.[53] Sleep deprivation is associated with more severe diseases like heart disease, risk of cancer, weight gain, Alzheimer's disease, and more. Sleep deprivation lowers performance, productivity, rational decision-making, memory recall, emotional control, and immune system function.[54] According to the National Center for Biotechnology, 75 percent of those who suffer from depression also suffer from a lack of sleep.[55] Studies also show that sleep deficiency

---

53 "Why We Sleep: Unlocking the Power of Sleep and Dreams," Booktable, accessed May 14, 2020.

54 "Sleep—The New Wonder Pill for Health and Happiness," Saltuary, accessed May 10, 2020.

55 D. Nutt, S. Wilson, and L. Paterson, "Sleep Disorders as Core Symptoms of Depression," *Dialogues in Clinical Neuroscience* 10, 3 (September 2008): 329–36, accessed May 13, 2020.

alters activity in some parts of the brain, which will lead to impaired memory and alertness.[56]

A study by the department of neurology at the University of Pennsylvania showed that good sleep can improve concentration, productivity, and performance. It also enhances our ability to learn, memorize, and make logical decisions. It recalibrates our emotions, restocks our immune system, fine-tunes our metabolism, and regulates our appetite. Sleep enhances our memory and makes us more creative. It helps you feel happier, less depressed, and less anxious.[57] In a nutshell, what all the research is trying to tell us is that good quality sleep is good for your health and for your productivity. Getting into a routine that allows for good sleep is important because it will enable you to execute on your goals more effectively.

So how do you improve your sleep habits? Here are some tips recommended by the National Heart, Lung, and Blood Institute[58]:

- Go to bed and wake up at the same time every day, even on weekends. Staying up late and sleeping in late on weekends can disrupt your body clock's sleep-wake rhythm.

---

56   "Scientists Find Brain Areas Affected By Lack Of Sleep," Society for Neuroscience, *ScienceDaily*, accessed May 16, 2020.

57   P. Alhola and P. Polo-Kantola, "Sleep Deprivation: Impact on Cognitive Performance" *Neuropsychiatric Disease and Treatment* 3, 5 (October 2007): 553–67, accessed May 6, 2020.

58   "Sleep Deprivation and Deficiency," National Heart, Lung, and Blood Institute, accessed May 8, 2020.

- Use the hour before bed for quiet time and try to avoid strenuous exercise and bright artificial light, such as from a TV or computer screen.
- Avoid having a large meal within a couple hours of bedtime, as well as any alcohol, nicotine, or caffeine. The effects of caffeine can last as long as eight hours, which means a cup of coffee in the late afternoon can make it hard for you to fall asleep at night.

Hopefully these tips can help you improve your quality of sleep. Having good sleep habits will certainly allow you to leverage the benefits of good sleep, which will prime you well to take massive action toward the achievement of your goals. Getting good sleep should be a habit right at the top of your list.

You should not end with establishing and implementing a good sleep routine. To ensure that you have the energy to go the distance, you must exercise regularly and eat healthy, good-for-you foods. Having good nutrition habits will help you improve your overall well-being. A proper diet helps prevent a wide range of health problems, plays a major role in ensuring you have the energy needed to achieve your goals and purpose, and sets you on track to attain fulfillment.

YOU ARE WHAT YOU EAT

Nutrition is one area you will need to focus on if you want to execute at the highest level. Do not neglect this area. The food you eat provides your body with the nutrition and energy it needs to function, so what we eat and when we eat directly affect our productivity and energy levels. Personally,

I found that both following an intermittent fasting schedule (I usually only eat solid foods from noon to 8:00 p.m.) and, although I still do eat meat, having a heavily plant-based diet give me the best energy. Since we are all different, I recommend getting professional help so you understand what works best for you nutritionally. However, the bottom line is for you to find the optimal eating habits that give you the best nutrition and energy so you can execute at the highest level.

Now that we have covered all the things you need to do to take action and execute toward your goals, we can now dive into the next stage of the S.P.E.A.R. method: **achieve**.

PART FOUR

ACHIEVE

CHAPTER 10

ATTITUDE DETERMINES ALTITUDE

———

Ability is what you're capable of doing. Motivation determines what you do. Attitude determines how well you do it.

—LOU HOLTZ

The Book of Galatians says, "A man reap what he sows."[59] Newton's third law of motion states, "For every action, there is an equal and opposite reaction."[60] You see, all the actions (or inactions) that we take will result in a correlated outcome. Ideally, setting a goal, creating a plan, and taking action would result in the desired outcome you want. In some cases, that is what happens. But life is rarely that straightforward. Even if you have the perfect plan and take all the necessary action steps, chances are you will encounter unexpected twists and turns on the road to any achievement.

———

59   Gal. 6:7 (New International Version).

60   "Newton's Third Law of Motion," Khan Academy, accessed April 27, 2020.

Success

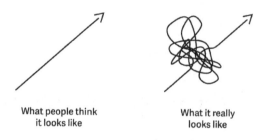

What people think
it looks like

What it really
looks like

Figure 10.1

You have spent time **seeking** your why, developing a **plan** and investing time and effort to **execute** the plan. As you work to **achieve** your goal, when unexpected twists and turns are thrown at you, maintaining a positive attitude will help you navigate yourself to success.

In 2005, by maintaining a positive attitude, Liverpool FC pulled off what is now dubbed the Miracle of Istanbul. Liverpool FC was playing AC Milan in the UEFA Champions League, the most prestigious club soccer trophy. AC Milan came out swinging and scored in the very first minute of the game. Things got even worse. By half-time, Liverpool FC was 3–0 down—talk about an unexpected twist if you were a Liverpool FC player or supporter. I remember feeling sorry for my father, a die-hard Liverpool supporter since the 1970s, watching his team take a beating. Everyone expected things to get worse in the second half. But Liverpool FC came back in the second half and enacted one of the most remarkable turnarounds in soccer history by scoring three goals in six minutes. With the game tied at 3–3 at the end of regular time, Liverpool FC went on to win the penalty shootout and with it the UEFA Champions League trophy. I remember Pat Nevin, former soccer player and now broadcast sports commentator, mentioning that Liverpool FC's positive attitude when the team was 3–0 down was key to its comeback. Being down such a margin at that time, some teams would have given up.

The **achieve** stage of the S.P.E.A.R. method is about making sure you get the most out of your journey to success. It is about digging in and doubling down. When things get tough, you will need to leverage your network to help you achieve your goal. It is about having a positive attitude amid mayhem. Only by so doing will you be able to navigate the unexpected twists and turns that will come up as you take action toward your goal. This stage is about catalyzing your actions so you achieve success more quickly. And, more importantly, it is about who you need to become to achieve the goal, which is more important than the actual goal itself.

Remember that the first, and probably most important, achievement is taking that first step outside your comfort zone and taking action toward your goal. By just doing this, you have already achieved a key milestone in your journey to success. You should not end at the first step but instead keep taking steps until you achieve your goal.

Given that unexpected twist and turns will come up while you are working toward your goal, maintaining a positive attitude will help you handle whatever life throws your way. Your attitude impacts everything: your thoughts, the energy you put out into the world, and most importantly, the actions you take. Your attitude toward any given situation influences the outcome of that situation when everything is said and done. Maintaining a good attitude can be the difference between living your fullest or just living a mediocre life without making the most of the time and gifts you have been given.

ATTITUDE IS EVERYTHING

If I have met a person who leverages the power of having a positive attitude and accomplishes things that many would have thought impossible, it is Sean Callagy. I first met Sean at an event in Rhinebeck, New York, where we were sampling our first batch of Nunbelievable cookies (a mission-based baked goods company I cofounded). We were getting ready to hand out the cookies in a barn when Sean and three guests walked in. Sean asked what was going on and we told him we were getting ready to hand out cookie samples. He asked if they could sample the cookies and we gave them some to try. As soon as Sean tasted our double chocolate cookie, he said, "This is the most delicious cookie I have ever tried. And I have tried a lot of cookies. Can we make a video about it right now?"

When we started recording the video, I noticed something about Sean—something strange about the way he was looking at me, as if he were not looking directly at me but past me. I wasn't sure what it was, but I could tell something was off. When we were done recording the video and they were leaving, I saw that Sean was guided out of the barn by his son, Tyler. At that point I realized Sean had impaired vision. Later that day, I learned Sean is legally blind due to retinitis pigmentosa, a rare disease he was diagnosed with when he was young that causes certain cells in the retina to start to die. As of now, the genetic disease, which his grandfather also had, has no cure. I also learned that Sean was a good baseball player in high school and at Columbia University. He was good enough to play professionally and was just a phone call away from being drafted in the 1992 MLB draft. The MLB team scouts had taken note of the ball drops he had made due to his vision problems and the draft call never came. And with that, his dream of being a professional baseball player never came true.

Now imagine if you were in Sean's shoes—slowly losing your vision while in high school and knowing you were fighting against the clock and your days of sight were numbered. How would you deal with the fact that at some point you will not be able to enjoy things like playing catch with your son or watching your daughter play soccer? What would your attitude toward life be if this were the hand life dealt you?

Well, Sean did not let this setback hold him back. Inspired by what happened with the "miracle on ice" (when the US men's ice hockey team defeated the defending gold medalist, the Soviet Union, at the 1980 Winter Olympics), Sean knew that with the right attitude he would be able to overcome his challenge and achieve great things in life. After missing out on the MLB draft, he decided to go to law school at Seton Hall University. After graduating law school, he landed a job with a prestigious law firm. Not happy with his job, he decided to take a risk and start his own law firm while he was still in his twenties.

Today, Sean is the founder and president of Callagy Law, a law firm with over one hundred team members, and has recovered over $300 million for health care providers in unpaid and underpaid claims from insurance carriers. Sean is one of only two attorneys out of more than a million attorneys in the United States to achieve two Top 100 National Jury Verdicts between 2014 and 2016, and the only one who was legally blind.[61] Sean has learned not to take anything in life for granted. He is persistent and pushes himself to be the best he can be and make a difference in other people's lives. Since our first meeting in Rhinebeck, I have had the privilege of spending time with Sean, and as we have connected more, I have learned some of his secrets to maintaining a positive attitude, one of which is his daily rituals. Each morning, Sean starts the day with gratitude by saying the things he is thankful for, followed by affirmation statements. Sean has also developed a self-mastery formula that he follows daily that enables you to influence yourself in your thoughts, actions, emotions, and state. The formula focuses on fourteen elements, such as self-awareness, journaling, values and rules, and focus. This self-mastery formula is part of the UNBLINDED Academy program. By following this daily routine, Sean is able to maintain a positive attitude, which he credits with helping him find solutions where others could only see obstacles.

Studies show that having a positive attitude can help us deal with stress, improve our overall well-being, and even boost our immune system. Furthermore, a recent study of 240 students done by the Stanford School of Medicine showed that having a positive attitude can positively impact our ability to

---

61 "Sean Callagy," Callagy Law, accessed June 1, 2020.

learn and solve problems.[62] By reviewing MRI brain scans to examine the neurological impact of positivity, the researchers found that students with a positive attitude toward math performed better in the subject compared to students with a negative attitude toward it.

According to a Stanford Research Institute study, the path to success consists of 88 percent attitude and only 12 percent education.[63] To be honest, I consider one's ability to positively control their attitude a life hack. Fostering a positive attitude manifests positive thinking that will enable you to see opportunities where others—people with a negative attitude—see problems. The classic glass-half-full or glass-half-empty litmus test can help you determine if you are an optimist or a pessimist by nature. Psychologist Suzanne Segerstrom, a professor of psychology and author of *Breaking Murphy's Law: How Optimists Get What They Want and Pessimists Can Too*, is known for her clinical research on optimism. One of her studies found that ten years after graduation, law students who were optimistic earned an average of $32,667 more than their glass-half-empty peers.[64] The results from this study are interesting because you can conclude that seeing the glass as half full makes you wealthier.

This is not the only study out there that has shown the benefits of being an optimist. Another research study conducted

62 Erin Digitale, "Positive attitude toward math predicts math achievement in kids," *Stanford University Medicine News*, January 24, 2018.

63 Timothy Reierson, "Attitude to Succeed," *Accountancy Student Blog* (blog), College of Business at Illinois, April 22, 2016.

64 Margie Warrell, "See the Glass Half Full Or Empty? Why Optimists Are Happier, Healthier & Wealthier!" *Forbes*, September 29, 2012.

by Dr. Martin Seligman, widely considered the father of positive psychology, also found that pessimistic people tend to make less money compared to their optimistic peers.[65] In his book *Learned Optimism*, Dr. Seligman found that optimists get sick less than pessimists.[66] Another study found optimism boosts your immune system by tracking changes in optimism and immune response among first-year law students.[67] A study published in 2010 in the *Journal of Thoracic Oncology* (JTO) discovered that lung cancer patients who exhibited an optimistic disposition experienced more favorable outcomes than those with a pessimistic disposition, thus showing that living life as an optimist leads to a healthier life. The researchers performed a retrospective evaluation of 534 adults diagnosed with lung cancer who had completed an assessment about eighteen years before receiving their lung cancer diagnosis between 1997 and 2006. Patients (both women and men) classified as having an optimistic attitude survived an average of six months longer compared to the patients with a pessimistic attitude. Five-year survival rates for the two groups were 32.9 percent for nonpessimists and 21.1 percent for pessimists.[68]

65   Martin E. Seligman and Peter Schulman, "Explanatory Style as a Predictor of Productivity and Quitting Among Life Insurance Sales Agents," *Journal of Personality and Social Psychology*, 50(4) (1986): 832–838.

66   Ciro Conversano, Alessandro Rotondo, Elena Lensi, Olivia D. Vista, Francesca Arpone, & Mario A. Reda, "Optimism and Its Impact on Mental and Physical Well-Being," *Clinical Practice and Epidemiology in Mental Health*, Vol. 6 (May 2010): 25-29.

67   Suzanne C. Segerstrom, "How Does Optimism Suppress Immunity? Evaluation of Three Affective Pathways," *Health Psychology*, 25(5) (Sep 2006): 653–657.

68   "Lung Cancer Patients with Optimistic Attitudes Have Longer Survival, Study Finds," International Association for the Study of Lung Cancer, *ScienceDaily*, accessed May 12, 2020.

When I read these studies on the benefits of having a positive attitude and being optimistic, I was immediately reminded of Hal Elrod and the SAVERS model (which you may recall from the last chapter). On December 3, 1999, at twenty years old, Hal was one of the top-producing sales reps for a multimillion-dollar marketing company. Driving his brand-new Ford Mustang around 11:00 p.m. down the freeway at seventy miles per hour, Hal was hit by a drunk driver in a Chevrolet truck traveling at an estimated eighty miles per hour. Following that impact, his car spun, and another Saturn sedan smashed into the driver's door at seventy miles per hour, leaving Hal severely injured. His brain was permanently damaged, he had eleven fractured bones, and after losing a lot of blood, he quickly plunged into a coma and was dead on the scene for six minutes before the medics were able to revive him. When he woke up from his coma six days later, Hal learned he might never walk again.

In such a situation, complaining and being pessimistic would be easy. One moment you are living your best life, and then the next, a drunk driver slams into your car and you are fighting for your life. But Hal decided to be optimistic and embraced his situation. His manager, Jesse Levine, had taught him the five-minute rule, which states, "It is okay to feel bad when something doesn't go according to plan, but not for more than five minutes." The rule allows you to yell, complain, or do whatever you feel like doing for five minutes. As soon as five minutes is up, you need to let it go and accept the situation as is, understanding the impossibility of changing the past and then focusing on what you need to do going forward. Hal had applied the five-minute rule many times before the car accident and did so while he was in the hospital bed to help him deal with his new reality and focus on creating a positive frame of mind. He understood he could do nothing to change the past, but he had the opportunity to influence his future.

Given his circumstance, Hal's optimism was a cause of concern for the doctors who spoke to his parents about it. By maintaining a positive outlook and focusing his mental energy on his goal, which was to walk again, Hal was able to overcome his situation and learn how to walk again after weeks of rehabilitation. The story gets even better, because not only did Hal learn how to walk again, but he also ran a fifty-two-mile ultramarathon. He returned to his sales rep job and had an amazing year, ranked sixth out of over sixty thousand active sales reps. In the spring of 2006, Hal published his first book, *Taking Life Head On: How to Love the Life You Have While You Create the Life of Your Dreams*, and since then has gone on to publish multiple best-selling books. His book *The Miracle Morning* has been translated into twenty-seven languages, and the SAVERS approach we discussed earlier is being practiced daily by over five hundred thousand people in over seventy countries.

A POSITIVE ATTITUDE CAN BE LEARNED

According to Dr. Seligman, we aren't born with a set explanatory style (being an optimist or pessimist) but rather are shaped by the people who we learn from as we grow up like our parents and our teachers. The good thing revealed by Dr. Seligman's studies is that optimism can be learned.

So how do you learn to be optimistic? A 2011 study by researchers at Maastricht University showed that engaging in a five-minute thought exercise of positive thinking can significantly increase your optimism. In the study, participants wrote about their best possible self for only five minutes in one of three domains: personal, relational, or professional. They repeated this exercise every day for two weeks, with the effects on optimism and mood measured after one session, after one week, and after two weeks. Compared to a control group, participants performing this exercise showed marked increase in their optimism and also experienced a more positive mood.[69]

This is why, when we were designing the #ThisIsMyEra 90-day planner, we decided to add a daily gratitude section and a daily positive affirmation statement section. What #ThisIsMyEra planner users have found after using the planner consistently for a couple of weeks is that by adding these positive thinking journaling tasks to their daily routines, they see a boost in optimism, overall mood, and self-confidence. By writing down positive reminders every day, you trigger feelings of happiness that will go a long way in cultivating optimism in your life.

Another way to cultivate optimism recommended by Dr. Jason Selk is to focus on solutions and not problems.[70]

69 Y.M.C. Meevissen, M.L. Peters, and H.J.E.M. Alberts, "Become More Optimistic by Imagining a Best Possible Self: Effects of a Two Week Intervention," *Journal of Behavior Therapy and Experimental Psychiatry* 42 (3) (Sep 2011): 371–78.

70 Jason Selk, "7 Ways to Become A More Optimistic Person," *Mindbodygreen* (blog), accessed May 7, 2020.

Obsessing over the problem tends to breed negative feelings and self-doubt. So, as you are working on your goals and facing obstacles, focusing on the problem is a much less productive use of your time and energy than focusing on potential solutions. Switching from problem-focused to solution-focused thinking gives you a sense of possibility and hope—key foundations for optimism. However, you should not ignore the problem all together. You simply must acknowledge that the problem exists and that problems are inevitable, but they are also temporary. Spending your time and energy focused on the solution is better than contemplating the actual problem.

Thomas Edison is a great example of someone who was solution-focused. His famous quote, "I have not failed. I've just found ten thousand ways that won't work," highlights that he was not centered on the problem but rather on identifying the solution. I am not sure how many people will be optimistic after failing ten thousand times while attempting to achieve a goal.

YOUR VIBE ATTRACTS YOUR TRIBE

While I was working on coming to the United States for college, I purposefully stopped talking to a lot of people I used to hang around before because I didn't want to be surrounded by their negative energy. They used to tell me I was wasting my time and that my dream of coming to the United States was impossible. Some even went as far as saying I was a fool. When I turned down an opportunity to study at a university in Zimbabwe, some even called me asking me if I had gone mad and if I was on drugs. I was fortunate enough to have a supportive family and a few friends who remained optimistic in a very challenging time. They became positive influences and energized me to keep moving along to find a breakthrough.

One of these friends was Bernard Londoni. In 2001, Bernard and his family escaped the war in the Democratic Republic of the Congo (DRC) after a rebel group attacked their village. Bernard lost his father during that attack. After refugee camps in other countries did not have capacity to accommodate them, Bernard and his remaining family found their way to Zimbabwe. The war had disrupted their life. Having arrived in Zimbabwe with nothing but their lives, they had to start building their lives from scratch. Bernard and his family had to learn English and Shona, the languages spoken in Zimbabwe, because they spoke French and Lingala (the DRC's native language).

As a refugee with minimal options at his disposal, Bernard did not give up on his dream of pursuing a US education. I met Bernard when he was also applying to schools in the United States, and we helped each other through the application process. Given what Bernard had experienced, I really admired his positive outlook to life. He did not let his past dictate his future and became a source of inspiration.

In August 2005, Bernard and I were on the same flight to Miami, Florida, both headed to Lynn University, where we studied together. Bernard had been awarded the presidential scholarship, which covered all college expenses. After graduating from Lynn, Bernard went on to successfully pursue a PhD from the School for Conflict Analysis and Resolution at

George Mason University. Dr. Londoni now works in Annapolis, Maryland, for an intelligence company focused on the Africa region.

Maintaining a positive attitude all the time can be difficult. Surrounding yourself with positive-minded people will help tremendously. If you are surrounded by people with negative attitudes, you will have great difficulty remaining positive because you are in a toxic ecosystem.

Make it a habit to maintain a positive attitude as you work to achieve success and fulfillment in your life. At times, we have no control over the cards we are dealt, but we do have control of our attitude. We can see many great examples, like Sean Callagy and Hal Elrod, of people who have managed to reach great levels of success and fulfillment by leveraging their positive attitude to help them navigate very challenging situations. Having a positive attitude will add tremendous value and can be the difference-maker as you pursue your goals.

You will also find that, as you venture out to achieve a goal, you need others to join you in that quest. Partnering up with people to help you achieve your goals is something that can accelerate your journey to the achievement of your goal. Mentors and accountability partners can also prove to be great allies. In the next chapter, we will focus on how collaboration is key to the achievement of your goals.

CHAPTER 11

COLLABORATE, COLLABORATE, COLLABORATE

If you want to go fast, go alone. If you want to go far, go together.
—AFRICAN PROVERB

In real estate, the property value is highly influenced by the principle "location, location, location." A house in the wrong location would not command the same value as that same house in the right location. When it comes to achieving goals, how far and how quickly you go toward achieving your goal can be determined by the principle "collaborate, collaborate, collaborate."

A strong case can be made that either Larry Page or Sergey Brin, the founders of Google, would not have been able to build Google to where it is today if they had not collaborated. Procter and Gamble reported $67 billion in revenue in its 2019 annual report.[71] Its household brands like Gillette, Pampers, Tide, Charmin, Old Spice, and Crest touch the lives of millions of consumers worldwide every day. None of this success would be possible if William Procter and James Gamble had not decided to collaborate in 1837.[72] Likewise, by collaborating, the Wright Brothers gifted the world flight in 1903. Elton John may not have sold over three hundred million records without collaborating with lyricist and song-writer Bernie Taupin.[73] Clearly, through collaboration, great feats can be achieved.

When you look at the list of the seventeen United Nations Sustainable Development Goals (SDGs), which provides a snapshot of the world's most pressing challenges, one can quickly realize that a single person or organization cannot solve these global issues. Personally, I am passionate about the fourth SDG: quality education. In 2018, the UN reported that over 260 million children were still out of school.[74] The goal is to ensure that all children have free, equitable, and quality primary and secondary education by 2030. To achieve this goal, governments, corporations, and individuals are going to need to collaborate.

Seeing the benefits of collaboration, many corporations are creating more open work spaces (breaking down the walls) and organizing talent into cross-functional teams. Research

---

71 "Annual Report 2019," Procter & Gamble, accessed May 6, 2020.

72 "Company History," Procter & Gamble, accessed May 6, 2020.

73 Elton John, "Elton John," accessed March 13, 2020.

74 "Sustainable Development—Education," United Nations, accessed March 12, 2020.

studies have provided evidence of the positive benefits of collaboration in the workplace, like helping solve problems faster, facilitating coworkers' learning from each other, and even boosting organizational morale.[75] A study that examined over 1,100 companies found that those promoting collaborative working were five times as likely to be high-performing.[76] Another study found that the mere perception of working collectively on a task can supercharge our performance.[77]

Collaboration is not just for the corporate world. You can leverage collaboration in your own success journey. In fact, I believe that if you plan to achieve anything meaningful in life, you need to get help from others, including partners, mentors, coaches, accountability partners, and more. Getting through the **achieve** stage of the S.P.E.A.R. method will require some form of collaboration, all based on what you are trying to achieve.

You may be asking, "How do I find people to collaborate with?" You can start by networking.

YOUR NETWORK IS YOUR NET WORTH

When I was at Tony Robbins's Business Mastery Event in West Palm Beach, Florida, over the course of a few days, I watched Gil Petersil perform a networking master class. The

---

75 Corey Moseley, "7 reasons why collaboration is important," *Jostle* (blog), accessed May 3, 2020.

76 Adi Gaskell, "New Study Finds That Collaboration Drives Workplace Performance," *Forbes*, June 22, 2017.

77 P. Carr and G. Walton, "Cues of Working Together Fuel Intrinsic Motivation," *Journal of Experimental Social Psychology* 53 (July 2014): 169–84.

man was on fire, as if almost all 2,500 attendees knew who he was even though he did not present anything on stage. He was bringing people together, getting people to connect during the breaks or after the day's session and providing value in a graceful way. I have never seen anyone connect with people in such an effective way (by the way, he rates himself a six out of ten on networking, on his best days).

So when I got a chance to talk to him one-on-one, I was not surprised to learn he was a networking mastery coach and serial entrepreneur. As an expert in the field of networking, Gil wrote a book called *New Code of Networking*. The book provides tips on how to build a network and better relationships.

In his early years as an entrepreneur, Gil had an epiphany. He learned that no one achieves anything meaningful on their own and that you always need the right people to help and support you. Part of this insight came from his earlier years. Gil was born in Israel and at age ten moved to Canada and could not speak English. The same thing happened ten years later, when he moved to Russia and he couldn't speak Russian. By learning how to build relationships and a network, he was able to successfully integrate in these new environments even with language barriers early on. With that insight, he decided to sharpen his networking skills and realized that effective networking helped him reach his goals more quickly and easily.

For many people, networking is terrifying. You go into a room full of strangers and try to strike up a conversation. For introverts, this task can be particularly challenging. I am talking from personal experience here. Once upon a time I would go to an event, hide in a corner, fidget on my phone, and only speak to people who came over to me. In my mind, I felt like I was Napoleon Dynamite watching all the cool kids make the most of their lives. People who know me now would not believe this. Over the years, I have learned to be a "situational extrovert"—my Myers-Briggs personality profile is ENTJ (extroverted, intuitive, thinking, judging), but I fell into the extroverted bucket literally by one mark.

Realizing I was wasting opportunities by not making the most of my attendance at an event, I started reading articles on how to network as an introvert and applied what I learned. One of the tips I took to heart is preparation. Before going to an event, I now prepare ahead of time. I try to find information about who is attending, who is organizing the event, and what the theme of the event is. Going to an event prepared increases my confidence and my comfort level, enabling me to bring my best self to the conversation. In situations where I do not know who will be attending ahead of time, I try to learn as much as I can about the event itself—for example, who is organizing it, whether there are any recaps from past events, and so on.

When I attended OC Impact (a convening of global leaders dedicated to building sustainable solutions organized by Opportunity Collaboration) in October 2018 as a Cordes Fellow, I hired an intern to create profiles of all four hundred-plus attendees. I read through all profiles over a two-week period, and when I arrived in Cancun, Mexico, for the four-day summit, I knew who everyone was and how I could potentially add value to what they were working on.

Attendees ended up calling me "Magic Kuda" because they were shocked by how well-prepared I was when we would meet. My preparedness for the OC Impact event helped me network effectively, which has led to my being invited to join boards, partnering up with other organizations, finding mentors who have guided me in achieving some ambitious goals, and building relationships that will last a lifetime.

Learning how to master the art of networking virtually is going to be an essential skill for the future. The recent COVID-19 pandemic may very well have accelerated the need to master this skill, so I highly encourage you to start looking into how you can prepare for a different reality when it comes to networking.

In the book *Networking Like a Pro*, author Ivan Misner, PhD, states that networking is about nurturing mutually beneficial relationships.[78] When done skillfully, networking can not only open doors to new opportunities but also connect you with the people and resources who can help you achieve your goal. I want to stress that you should go into the conversation with an authentic paradigm and truly nurture the relationship. One cardinal mistake many people make is going into it only thinking about what they can get out of the relationship. They ask for a favor too soon, which is like proposing marriage on the first date. Asking for a favor too soon can damage the relationship you are trying to build. Find ways you can provide value and give first before you can get. Think of it as a bank account: you want to make a deposit into

---

78 "Network Like A Pro," Joseph Jude, accessed April 27, 2020.

the relationship first so you have a positive account balance before you withdraw from it.

Do not go to networking events just to collect business cards. Once you have established a connection with someone, you need to follow up. After making a connection, too many people drop the ball and fail to follow up to nurture the relationship. Author and professional relationship expert Keith Ferrazzi encourages connecting with your network regularly.[79] He suggests scheduling time in your calendar so you do not let this step slide through the cracks.

When I moved to New Jersey, I set a goal to connect in person with as many people in my network as possible who lived in the area. When I met Lauren Cecchi, my college friend, for dinner, little did I know that our dinner conversation would lead to us partnering in a business venture. Lauren and I met in college when I was a junior and the resident assistant (RA) in a freshman residence hall. Lauren and her friends, who were freshmen at the time, were making noise late one night and I was the RA on duty. Although our first encounter was not the typical networking meet, Lauren and I connected. Both of us had a knack for business, and we kept tabs on each other through college. When I created AFR Clothing in college, Lauren and her mother were my very first customers when we launched at the Lynn University fashion show.

While we were at dinner, Lauren shared with me a side project in sports collectibles she was working on that had hit a

---

79   Molly Triffin, "8 Secrets from Power Networking Pros," *Forbes*, July 23, 2014.

standstill. Lauren and her father had managed to secure a patent on a collectible idea they had for memorabilia pieces with an authentic autograph or digital signature and had even gone as far as creating prototypes with a manufacturer. However, her Lauren Cecchi New York luxury handbag line was gaining traction. The line was now being carried by Macy's, and she was going through the growing pains that made it hard for her to work on the side project.

As an avid sports fan, I was so fascinated by her side project. I felt the concept she and her father created had massive potential. I was so excited that we left dinner almost immediately and went to her apartment to look at the prototypes.

After seeing the prototypes, I knew I could help her bring this product to market. The product concept required acquiring licenses with sports franchises. When I finished my MBA, I was hired by Jarden Consumer Solutions, a subsidiary of Jarden Corporation (now a part of Newell Brands—NYSE: NWL) in its recently formed Transformational Innovation Group. In that role, I was responsible for creating new disruptive businesses for the company. One of the businesses I launched was a meal delivery service for slow-cooker meals called Crock-Pot Cuisine.

To scale the business, I worked closely with our licensing team to form a strategic alliance with Omaha Steaks. Through that, I had gained experience on how licensing deals work and built strong relationships with licensing experts. By tapping into those relationships, we were able to find our way to the negotiation table with Paris Saint-Germain Football Club, the best soccer team in France. Once we had secured that licensing deal, we were able to quickly add Chelsea FC, Liverpool FC, Manchester City FC, and Arsenal FC—top English teams and powerhouses in the soccer world—to the lineup.

A few months after securing the licensing deals, we launched our new business called Signables at a sports tradeshow in Las Vegas attended by sporting goods retailers—the perfect place to network with buyers. By networking and collaborating, Lauren and I were able to achieve the goal of launching a new business into the marketplace. If we had not kept in touch and decided to collaborate, Signables may have never been launched and sports fans would have missed out on the joy the product gives them. I am amazed when I see pictures of happy customers with their Signables. As a Chelsea FC fan, when I first saw our product in the Chelsea Megastore at Stamford Bridge (the Chelsea stadium store), I cried. Words cannot express how I feel having the privilege of creating officially licensed merchandise with my beloved sports team for fans just like me. All these achievements were made possible through collaboration.

WE ALL NEED A MR. MIYAGI

The Karate Kid was one of the first movies I watched when we got our first color TV and VHS player in the early nineties. I loved that movie so much that I watched it almost every weekend for a few months. In the film, Daniel, the Karate Kid, had just moved to California from New Jersey with his mother. The teenager struggles to fit in, and a group of bullies make his life a living hell. He meets Mr. Miyagi, a master martial artist, when Mr. Miyagi saves Daniel from the group of bullies beating him. Mr. Miyagi then trains Daniel for an upcoming karate tournament, in which Daniel would fight his worst bully. Through the training process, Mr. Miyagi not only trains Daniel for the upcoming fight but also takes Daniel under his wing and mentors him, teaching him many important life lessons. Daniel makes it to the final of the karate tournament and with an injured leg and defeats his arch-bully to win the tournament. Having a mentor helped Daniel achieve a great feat and also helped him grow and learn many life lessons.[80]

One of the ways to help you achieve success more quickly, go farther, and make fewer mistakes is having a mentor. The origins of mentoring can be traced back to ancient Greece. Socrates mentored Plato. Plato went on to mentor Aristotle. Aristotle then mentored Alexander the Great.[81]

Steve Jobs and Mark Zuckerberg are a modern example of a famous mentor-mentee relationship. In 2011, when Steve Jobs passed away, Mark Zuckerberg posted, "Steve, thank you for being a mentor and a friend. Thanks for showing that what you build can change the world. I will miss you." Zuckerberg relied on Jobs's mentorship as Facebook grew. In an interview with *Business Insider*, Zuckerberg shared the advice Jobs once gave him when he had hit a rough patch and a lot of people wanted to buy Facebook. Jobs's advice to Zuckerberg was to reconnect with what he believed was the

---

80 *The Karate Kid*, directed by John Avildsen, featuring Macchio, Ralph, and Morita, Noriyuki (United States: Columbia Pictures, 1984), VHS.

81 Samuel Osho, "5 Powerful Mentoring Relationships that Influenced the World," *Samosho* (blog), August 12, 2018.

mission of the company, which helped Zuckerberg make the decision on what to do during that tough time.[82]

Real estate maverick and best-selling author Kris Krohn said, "Mentors are the most important key to success. My success is directly tied to my mentors' guidance. Without my mentors, I wouldn't be the man I am today."[83] At one point in his life, Krohn did not have money to provide for his family, but through real estate investing, he was able to become financially independent and retire at twenty-six years old. Mentoring has been a major part of his success. He recommends finding someone who has already been where you want to be and follow in their footsteps.

If having a traditional one-on-one mentorship relationship with someone you admire is something that's not possible, you can still get mentorship by reading books and even following the person on their social platforms. I have learned a lot from reading blogs and following social media platforms of successful people I admire. Krohn himself provides real estate mentorship to people through his YouTube channel, which has more than half a million subscribers.

Another great example is Strive Masiyiwa's Facebook page, where he shares business lessons he has learned over the years. I follow both Strive Masiyiwa and Kris Krohn, and the knowledge they share on their platforms is pure gold. In fact,

---

82 Jillian D'Onfro, "Mark Zuckerberg says that visiting an Indian temple at the urging of Steve Jobs helped him stick to Facebook's mission," *Business Insider*, September 27, 2015.

83 Kris Krohn, "Mentors are the most important key to success..." Facebook, May 21, 2020.

I would go as far as saying the information they share is more practical and more valuable than an MBA. Now, what you do with this information once you get it is what can be the difference between you achieving your goal or not. Remember, knowledge is potential power. Applying that knowledge is where the true power lies.

A survey by the American Society for Training and Development reported that 75 percent of executives say mentoring has been critical to their career development.[84] So taking the time to find and connect with a mentor will help accelerate your path to success. Having worked with a few mentors, I have benefited from their constructive criticism and ability to point out blind spots that would have resulted in disastrous outcomes.

If you cannot find a mentor who has been there and done that, finding an accountability partner can be a great alternative. An accountability partner is someone who can hold you accountable for your actions. A great accountability partner can help you make significant progress toward the achievement of your goal. Research studies have shown that publicly committing to your goals in front of someone gives you at least a 65 percent chance of completing them. However, having a specific accountability partner increases your chance of success to 95 percent.[85]

---

84 Alyssa Rapp, "Be One, Get One: The Importance of Mentorship," *Forbes*, October 2, 2018.

85 Thomas Oppong, "Psychological Secrets to Hack Your Way to Better Life Habits," *Observer*, March 20, 2017.

Even the brilliant Isaac Newton recognized the value of involving others in your journey to success. I love this quote by him: "If I have seen further than others, it is by standing upon the shoulders of giants." So, in your quest to achieve great things, be sure to bring in other people to help you get there. Mentors provide a great way to tap into the wisdom of others, which can help you avoid mistakes. You can also partner with people who are strong in the areas you are weak. Having someone share the load with you is always good. As they say, two heads are better than one.

What goals and dreams are you potentially missing out on by not collaborating with others? Take some time to think of people you can collaborate with and help with their goals and then think of people who can help you. It's a two-way street, so always think about how you can provide value first and then think about what value you need. Take some time to find events you can attend to network and make new connections. Remember—your net worth is your network.

Please exercise due diligence as you make decisions on who to collaborate with or who you get to mentor you. Some people may not be the best people to partner with. Take your time learning about the person to see if you are a fit for each other. Be wise. Bad partnerships can lead to failure.

In Africa, they say it takes a village to raise a child. Perhaps you are being held back from your goal by not collaborating with others or vice versa—someone is waiting for you to reach out so you can help them achieve their dreams. So, go out there and collaborate.

CHAPTER 12

PERSEVERANCE MAKES DREAMS COME TRUE

———

Perseverance, secret of all triumphs.

—VICTOR HUGO

Not everyone who starts a race finishes it. Some will take the time to seek their why, prepare their game plan, and take the first few action steps to execute the plan, yet somewhere along the way they will get discouraged, give up, and fail to achieve their desired goal. Then certain others—like Thomas Edison, who persevered even after failing ten thousand times—continue until they meet their goal and finally light up the world. Edison wisely said, "Many of life's failures are people who did not realize how close they were to success when they gave up." No matter how talented or gifted you are, success will always require a good dose of perseverance.

COMING TO AMERICA

Since I was nine years old, my dream was to leave Zimbabwe after high school and study abroad, preferably at a US university. This dream was sparked after my encounter with Sara. I wanted to use my education to create businesses that I would leverage to change lives across the world, starting with those in my home country. When I got to high school, I started looking into ways to make this dream happen. I was aware it would be a long shot since, coming from a lower middle-class family, my parents couldn't possibly afford to pay the tuition at a US university. At that time, the National Center for Education Statistics reported that the average total cost, including tuition, fees, room, and board, at a four-year institution (both public and private) was $20,218, with private institutions averaging at was $32,690.[86] My parents simply didn't have that kind of money.

To make matters even worse, in 2003, the Zimbabwean economy was experiencing hyperinflation. Unemployment was high, since many companies were forced to shut down due to the tough economic conditions and skyrocketing inflation. World Data reported the 2003 inflation rate in Zimbabwe as 432 percent.[87] The US inflation rate during that same period was 2.3 percent.[88] Gone were the good old days when Zimbabwe used to be considered the breadbasket of Africa, exporting wheat, tobacco, and corn, among other products.

---

86 "Tuition Costs of Colleges and Universities," National Center for Education Statistics, accessed March 12, 2020.

87 "Development of inflation rates in Zimbabwe," World Data, accessed June 2, 2020.

88 "Current US Inflation Rates: 2009-2020," US Inflation Calculator, accessed June 2, 2020.

But things changed, and now the country barely produces enough to feed its own population. *Zimbabwe's* economic demise began in the 1990s and accelerated in the 2000s. The government's controversial decision to intervene in the Democratic Republic of the Congo's civil war in 1998 was a major accelerator, as it put a huge burden on the economy and also resulted in the suspension of international economic aid for the country.

The situation worsened in later years due to economic sanctions implemented on the country mainly because of a violent land reform program. This economic pressure made life difficult for the average Zimbabwean and made pursuing an education abroad almost impossible for students, especially if you did not have a full scholarship. These circumstances made my dream of getting a US college education sound like a Disney fantasy whenever I would share it with others. People would laugh at me and offer words of "wisdom." Some would even go as far as asking me to lower my expectations and be "realistic."

Since I had clarity on my why, I never allowed this criticism to stop me from dreaming and taking action. I was willing to take risks in pursuit of my why and not let fear stop me. In my heart of hearts, I knew that what seemed impossible could be made possible. So I transformed all the negative energy into fuel that propelled me to take massive action.

After high school graduation, I worked the night shift at an internet café to pay for my SAT exams, a membership at the US Educational Advising Center, and all the college application fees. I scored extremely well on my SATs and applied to nearly thirty universities in the United States. I also applied to schools in the United Kingdom, Australia, Russia, and South Africa as backup. In total, I applied to more than fifty institutions. College application essays became my life for about six months. I had no social life, as all my nonworking time was consumed by college applications. I would spend the entire day writing essays, researching, and filling out applications. I knew my golden ticket to an American education was a full-ride scholarship, but these are the most competitive. They are high in demand, from the best of the best in the world, and low in supply, so to increase my chances to get into one, I pretty much dedicated that era of my life to this.

In no time, schools started responding. After receiving five acceptances out of five responses, I was not any closer to my dream. None of the schools had given me a substantial scholarship. The average scholarship from the schools was about $5,000, while the average total tuition and room and board for these schools was about $40,000. That type of financial aid is not enough to get your visa approved, so I had to wait for the other schools to reply in the hopes that I would get better aid.

As I waited to hear back from more schools, my parents asked me to apply to a Zimbabwean institution just in case the trend of getting accepted and getting inconsiderable funding continued. Basically, they wanted me to have a plan B in case my plan of leaving the country did not work out. After weeks of pushing back, I decided to honor my parents' request and apply to one Zimbabwean university—the National University of Science and Technology (NUST).

Zimbabwe follows a similar education system to the British education system, so in my A Level studies (think of that as eleventh and twelfth grade in the United States), I focused on math, physics, chemistry, and computer science. Based on my concentration on science-based subjects, NUST was the ideal Zimbabwean university choice for me. I applied to its engineering program and got accepted. Ironically, I received multiple options to fully fund my tuition fees at NUST—exactly what I needed to happen with the US schools. Everyone I knew advised that I take the NUST offer and forget about the American dream. At this point, I was ten for ten with my US college applications, with the scholarship average still hovering around $5,000. Given that trend, it was a no-brainer to everyone: "better take what you have than let that go, hoping for something to come up" is what they would say. I must admit, they had a pretty solid argument based on the trends. They probably did not want to see me heartbroken in case my American dream never manifested after turning down NUST.

The day came to go to NUST to register for classes. At that time, two US schools were still yet to send their decisions. I had to make a call. After hours of debating with my parents, I gave in and took an overnight train ride to Bulawayo, the second largest city in Zimbabwe, where the NUST campus is located. My roommate-to-be, Michael Nyajeka, was thrilled to see me. He was hoping we would continue our streak as roommates, since he was my roommate in high school as boarders.

The plan was simple—go to NUST on day one to register for classes and use day two and three to hunt for an apartment and then go back home on day four. I would then spend a few weeks at home before starting school. Since I took the overnight train, I arrived in Bulawayo quite early and was one of the first students to complete registration. As I waited for Michael and other high school friends, I explored the campus and was quite pleased by it. I had two cousins who had graduated from NUST and I could see why they spoke highly of the institution. During this time of idleness, I started pondering some questions:

- *If I do come to NUST, am I giving up on my life's dreams?*
- *Will taking this step be in alignment with my life's purpose and being a force of good?*
- *Is this decision to come to NUST being driven by fear?*
- *Even if I do succeed at NUST, will I be fulfilled?*

The questions kept going back and forth in my head for about ten minutes. I was at a crossroads. I had to decide—either go to NUST and forever live with the consequences of giving up on my dream or turn down NUST and chase my American dream. At this point in my life, this decision was the toughest I'd ever had to make. In that moment, I reflected on the life-changing experience I had when I met Sara (the little girl who did not go to school) and how that had shaped my life's purpose. I reflected on the plan I had put together on how I would go to the United States and the countless hours I had invested executing the plan. But here I was with nothing to show for it. I had fought a good fight and maybe everyone was right—it was time for me to throw in the towel.

In that moment, I decided to call my dad and tell him I was going to focus on NUST and let the American dream go. I shared with him how I liked the campus and the city. What happened next was like a movie scene—in fact, very much like the scene from *The Wolf of Wall Street* when Jordan Belfort (played by Leonardo DiCaprio) is about to announce to his team that he's leaving the securities industry after striking a deal with federal agents. As he is giving the speech and comes to the part where he's supposed to say, "I am leaving," he flips the script and tells everyone he is staying. That's exactly what I did.

Right when I was about to tell my dad I was going to give up on my American dream and focus on getting my engineering degree at NUST, I flipped the script and told him I'd decided to follow my heart and was not going forward with NUST. In fact, I was headed to the train station right after the call to switch my ticket and return home that evening. An awkward silence ensued. To my surprise, my dad reacted in a way I was not expecting. His words were supportive. He simply said, "If that is what you want, then that's what Mum and Dad want too. See you tomorrow."

The long train ride back gave me time to reflect on my decision. Had I just sacrificed an amazing opportunity? What I did not know on the ride back home was exactly how much this decision was going to require of me in terms of both time and effort. A few weeks after turning down NUST, one of the two remaining schools sent their acceptance letter with no scholarship grant accompanying the admissions offer. So everything was now hanging on the one remaining school: Lynn University.

When its decision letter came in, you can imagine the anticipation everyone had. The entire American dream was riding on this letter. Lynn University came through and gave me a lifeline. It was not the full-ride Presidential Scholarship I was hoping for, but the school did award me the Dean's Scholarship, which covered 50 percent of my needs. This offer was the best I had received, and it was the last school to send its decision, so I had to go on a quest to find the other 50 percent. I applied to every scholarship I could find that I qualified for. I found more than two hundred of them. I wrote hundreds of letters to corporations, nonprofits, philanthropists, entrepreneurs, and more. However, all these efforts proved to be in vain because I was not able to secure any funding by the time school started, and I had to defer my entry that year and use the time to find the money I needed.

I started a small business selling blank CDs imported from South Africa with the hope to save the profits. But the economic climate in Zimbabwe did not help. The high inflation rate and foreign currency shortage made it difficult to save. Plus, my business did not have the scale to generate the $20,000 I needed. I did not stop persevering and went back to searching for more scholarships and grants I could qualify for.

This period of my life tested my mental strength. My high school classmates were now in their second year at university. Whenever I would talk to them, they would subtly find a way to convey the "you should have listened to us" message. But I remained resolute in my quest and doubled down on my action. Two years had now passed since I'd made the decision not to go to NUST.

And then, at long last, I received a phone call that changed my life.

Hi Kuda, we have seen how much you have sacrificed for your dream to go to America and we decided to take out a loan to cover the balance needed for your freshman year at Lynn University," my sister Martha said on the other end of the line. She had moved to the United Kingdom a few years back and had literally just answered my years of prayer.

I stood there in shock, with no words to say.

I felt like saying thank you was not enough because what she had just done was such a big deal. It was life-changing. My sister was inspired by my perseverance and happy to take the financial risk for me because she believed I would not waste the opportunity. This phone call came in a few days before the semester started, so we had to move quickly to get my visa processed and plane ticket purchased, and just like that, I was going to the United States.

Through perseverance (and my sister's help), I finally achieved my goal of going to the United States for college. If I had given up, I would not have achieved my dream.

EVERY CHAMPION WAS ONCE A CONTENDER WHO REFUSED TO GIVE UP

Golden Globe Award winner Sylvester Stallone is well known for his role in the *Rocky* movie franchise that has earned over $1.5 billion at the box office, making it one of the most successful franchises of all time.[89] Stallone's dream was always to be an actor, but his previous acting roles had not brought the success he had hoped for. Although he was dead broke, he did not give up on his dream. Instead, he went all in. Stallone's financial situation got so severe that he was left with no choice but to sell his beloved dog. He did not have any money for food for himself or the dog. Out of options, he stood in front of a liquor store with his dog and sold it to a man for $25.

Given his desperate situation, Stallone could have easily given up on his acting dream, found a "real" job, and obtained a steady income. But doing so would have led to an unfulfilled life, since he knew he would not be following his life's calling. A few weeks after selling his dog, he saw a boxing match between Muhammad Ali and Chuck Wepner, and that was the fight that inspired him to write the script for the movie *Rocky*. Stallone wrote nonstop for three days until the script was done.

When he went out to sell the script, a studio offered him $125,000 for it. For someone who is dead broke, $125,000 is certainly life-changing. He was at a crossroads, unsure whether to take the money or chase the dream of being an actor—just like me when I was considering going to NUST or pursuing my dream. Stallone declined the offer because the studio was not willing to give in to his condition that he'd be the main actor in the movie.

---

89 *Rocky*. The Numbers, accessed May 3, 2020.

The studio producers felt that Stallone looked and talked funny and preferred to get Ryan O'Neal or Burt Reynolds for the role instead. A few weeks later, the studio increased its offer to $250,000. Stallone refused again. The company went on to increase the offer to $360,000.[90] Stallone still refused because the studio still did not give in to his request to be in the movie.

Finally, the studio agreed to give Stallone $35,000 and let him be the star in the movie. Although this sum was much lower than the initial offer, Stallone's dream of being an actor with a leading role in a movie came true. Once the deal was done, Stallone went back to liquor store where he had sold his dog to try and find the man he'd sold the dog to so he could buy his dog back. After waiting for a few days, the guy who had bought the dog finally showed up. The guy declined Stallone's offer to buy the dog back for $100. After going back and forth, the guy eventually agreed to sell the dog back to Stallone for $15,000 plus a feature in the movie.[91]

Since the studio felt it was taking a risk with Stallone as the lead actor, they decided to only give the movie a $1 million budget, which even in the 1970s was a low budget for a movie. The movie was a massive success. It went on to gross over $200 million on the box office, win three Oscars out of nine nominations, and become the foundation for the *Rocky* franchise we know today. If Stallone had given up on his dream, the world would have missed out on such an amazing movie

90 Tom Ward, "The Amazing Story of The Making Of 'Rocky,'" *Forbes*, August 29, 2017.

91 Melissa Chu, "Sylvester Stallone on fighting for what you want," *The Ladders*, April 10, 2020.

and life story. For me, the greatest takeaway from Sylvester Stallone's story is perseverance. To achieve your life's purpose or dream, you may very well find yourself in situations where perseverance and sacrifice will be what take you there.

Perseverance in pursuing your goal in spite of difficulty is fundamental to achieving success. As you work through the **achieve** stage, you will likely face hard times, and unexpected twists and turns will almost definitely come up. You may find yourself having to *sell that dog* to stay on track to achieve your goal. You may be tempted to quit, but sacrifice and perseverance can get you to the promised land.

My friend and serial entrepreneur Gary Nealon knows a little about perseverance. Gary's first business venture failed miserably. He bought a wholesale distribution business in the dollar store niche—right before the market crash of 2008. When the cost of petroleum rose sharply, the margins in the business disappeared completely and he had to file for bankruptcy. At the age of thirty and with only $5,000 to his name, Gary had to start all over again.

Given such an experience, others would shy away from venturing into business again and opt for less risky options. But not Gary. He took on another venture, this time a kitchen cabinet e-commerce business called RTA Cabinet Store. This move was rather risky considering consumers tend to buy kitchen cabinets at a hardware store like Home Depot and not online since they like to touch and feel the material. Gary managed to implement savvy digital marketing strategies that enabled him to drive traffic to his website.

As the business started to gain momentum, Gary knew the business's margin would go up by 30 percent if it added its own line of kitchen cabinets that were manufactured overseas in addition to the dropship model. So he and his business partner decided to proceed with this strategy. Since Gary did not fully know the ins and outs of this new supply chain model, Gary's business ran out of working capital and could not make payroll. Gary was now on the brink of filing for bankruptcy for the second time unless he could find a way to navigate this situation and get the business back on track.

After a few pivots, Gary was able to find the winning formula, and within a few years the business reached $40 million in revenue. Shortly after, he sold the business. If Gary had given up during the tough season that almost led to him filing bankruptcy, he would not have achieved his goal of a multimillion-dollar exit. His determination and willingness to preserve enabled him to finally achieve success.

GOAL ACHIEVED, NOW WHAT?

You have taken action, overcome the unexpected twists and turns that life throws at you, and persevered through hard times, and now the goal that seemed more like pipe dream is reality. Now what? Well, first things first, you should celebrate that milestone. Soak in the glory because you deserve it. But do not do it for long. Why? Because you have one more stage of the S.P.E.A.R method: **repeat**.

PART FIVE

REPEAT

CHAPTER 13

YOU CANNOT SURVIVE ON YOUR LAST BREATH

———

Instructions for successful living: Dream it. Plan it. Do it. Repeat.

—STEVE MARABOLI

Congratulations! You have achieved the goal you worked so hard for. Now what?

First, celebrate. Something once a dream is now a reality. You sharpened your blade, took aim, threw your spear, and hit the target. All the planning and executing has now paid off and you have achieved your goal, so go out, have a nice dinner with your loved ones, take a vacation, or spend the day at the spa. Do it because you have earned it. Celebrating accomplishments can boost your confidence, which in turn can fuel your continued success. Celebrating every success, big or small, will help cultivate your success mindset.

Celebrating is also a way to hack into your happy chemicals. Research shows us that you get a hit of dopamine when you celebrate.[92] This experience will play a part in your next goal. When you get a dopamine hit, your brain pays attention to what you did to earn your "feel-good" moment. So your brain will analyze what's needed to repeat that action and move toward achieving your next goals. As you can see, neuroscientific benefits accompany celebrating after reaching a goal that go beyond enjoying that current moment.

Now, once you are done celebrating, keep your foot on the pedal. Once you achieve success, you will experience temptation to just sit back and do nothing. Self-made millionaire Paul Scolardi said, "Sure, you have to enjoy life, but continue to use and improve the work ethic that helped you to achieve the success you now have." Instead of sitting back, leverage the greater confidence you now have from the recent achievement and set bigger goals.

Tony Robbins loves to say, "If you are not growing, you are dying." Once you achieve your goal, you should celebrate that milestone, but quickly go back to the drawing board and create an action plan for something even grander than the goal you have just achieved. If the goal you just achieved was a step toward your larger life's goal, that's great—now work on the next goal so you can get even closer to achieving your life's purpose. That's exactly what my wife did after she achieved her 5K goal. The next thing she did was sign up for a 10K race and also an obstacle course event. What

92   Erin Wildermuth, "The Science of Celebration: 5 Reasons Organizations Should Do It More Often," *Michael Hyatt* (blog), accessed May 13, 2020.

was great about this move was that she was able to apply the momentum she had from her 5K triumph toward two goals that were more challenging but totally in alignment with her why. The key is to maintain the momentum you have built from your achievement of the previous goal and have it propel you to the achievement of your next goal, which is why the last stage of the S.P.E.A.R method is **repeat**.

George Bernard Shaw put it best when he said, "I dread success. To have succeeded is to have finished one's business on earth, like the male spider, who is killed by the female the moment he has succeeded in his courtship. I like a state of continual becoming, with a goal in front and not behind." George Bernard Shaw knows a thing or two about always pursuing a new goal once you achieve the one you were working toward. In his lifetime, he wrote more than sixty plays and won many other awards, including the Nobel Prize. In 1950, Shaw died at the age of ninety-four while working on yet another play. Even at that age, he felt that as long as he was alive, he could still pursue a goal and not rest on past successes. That mindset is one we should all attempt to replicate.

MENTAL RESPIRATION

You see, in order to survive, you need to continuously inhale air so you supply your body with oxygen while exhaling used air out, in the form of carbon dioxide, since your body cannot use it. Humans, like many other aerobic creatures, need oxygen to make energy through a process called cellular respiration.[93] The Encyclopedia Britannica describes cellular

---

93   "Cellular Respiration," Khan Academy, accessed April 27, 2020.

respiration as the "process by which organisms combine oxygen with foodstuff molecules, diverting the chemical energy in these substances into life-sustaining activities and discarding, as waste products, carbon dioxide and water."[94] Cellular respiration will keep occurring unless the cell runs out of oxygen—hence the constant need to breathe.

The same is true with goals. Goals are the oxygen of our life's purpose. Similar to how our cells need energy derived from "cellular respiration" to perform vital life activities, our minds need energy derived from "mental respiration"—my way of defining the process by which one combines a goal with planning to generate the motivation (energy) required to trigger action in pursuit of the achievement of that goal.

Once that goal is achieved, another goal is required to fill in the place of the previous goal and trigger the same *mental respiration* process again, like how we need to continuously breathe to keep cellular respiration occurring so we stay alive. When you achieve your goal, you have not reached the end; attaining a goal simply opens the door to the next goal and gives you permission to start working on that next one. Remember the words of George Bernard Shaw from earlier: "a state of continual becoming."

Now, repeat. Once you achieve your goal, go back to seeking your next goal, then create a plan on how to achieve it, take the required action, and next thing you know, that goal is achieved and you are repeating the process again.

---

94   Encyclopaedia Britannica Online, s.v. "Cellular respiration," accessed April 6, 2020.

RENT IS DUE EVERY DAY

This notion of always being in a state of continual becoming was shared in an interesting way by my friend Liran Hirschkorn. He left his role as a bank manager to start a life insurance agency. He grew and sold that business. After that, he started selling on Amazon and has built multiple multi-million-dollar brands that derive most of their sales from Amazon. He recently started a new advertising agency that helps brands grow on Amazon. As a person who believes in enjoying success in all areas of life and not just in business, Liran has taken radical action to live a heathier life and spend more time with his family.

As I have witnessed Liran achieve multiple feats, I was curious about what keeps him going, why he keeps repeating the process of pursuing an even bigger goal after an achievement. Liran shared with me an inspiring quote I believe will guide you to repeatedly take action to achieve goals: "Success is never owned. It is rented. And the rent is due every day." The man credited for these words is bestselling author Rory Vaden.

The point Liran was making with those words was that far too often we see people rise to success by doing something amazing, only to see them fall off the radar completely because they became complacent and stopped doing things that took them to the top. They figure, *I reached this milestone—let me just kick back and take it easy,* and expect to still be at the top. No, life doesn't work like that. You must keep pushing.

Success is a temporary condition. You can be successful today and still fail tomorrow. To stay successful, you have to do the work every day. You have to pay the rent every single day. Do you think Usain Bolt or Michael Phelps would have dominated their sporting disciplines by not putting in the work daily? Do you think they would have won another gold medal by kicking back and relaxing because they won the previous Olympics? Achieving success is not easy, and maintaining it is even harder.

LEARN. EARN. RETURN.

I sit on the Council of Stakeholders for the Social Impact Lab at Lynn University, my alma mater. Ron Cordes, cochair of the council, brings the whole notion of mental respiration to life in an interesting way. As the cofounder and CEO, Ron helped build AssetMark to become a leading US managed account platform with $9 billion assets under management. In 2006, the company was sold to Genworth Financial for $230 million.[95] While many would have sat back and enjoyed retirement, he set a new goal and repeated the whole cycle to reach a new goal. Ron said, "I'd had this concept in college that the first third of your life was to learn, the second third was to earn, and the final third was to return."[96]

So after selling Assetmark, Ron and his wife, Marty, established a $10 million family foundation called the Cordes Foundation focused on social entrepreneurship as a way to

---

95 Caroline Fairchild, "How Ron Cordes Went from Profits to Purpose," *Fortune*, April 11, 2014.

96 "Ron Cordes: How to Make Your Second Career Count," Cordes Foundation, accessed May 29, 2020.

give back to society.[97] The foundation activates 100 percent of its balance sheet for impact by investing in mission-aligned opportunities across multiple asset classes with a gender lens investment strategy that seeks to deliver strong, risk-adjusted, market-rate financial returns because of its focus on social impact and not the lack thereof. Focusing on social impact investments has paid off for the Cordeses because their portfolio was able to come out of the 2008 financial crisis without a single loss since their investments were not tied to the global financial market. Believe it or not, Ron actually feels his second career not only has provided a fresh breath in his life, but also keeps him busier than his first career. More importantly, he is able to give to others through mentorship, advising, and also impact investing.

Truly, the first goal of Ron's life was to learn. Once that goal was achieved, he set his sights on earning, and once that goal was achieved, he then focused on returning what he has earned and changing lives in a meaningful way. Each stage gives Ron that breath that keeps him moving.

WIN A GOLD MEDAL IN ONE THING FIRST

The first time I met billionaire entrepreneur Jeff Hoffman was in December 2017, at a conference in Austin, Texas. Whenever you go to an airport and enjoy using a self-service check-in kiosk, you should thank Jeff. Out of frustration from standing in a line for close to an hour at the airport checking in, Jeff decided to solve this consumer pain point by

---

97 "Solving the World's Problems," Cordes Foundation, accessed May 29, 2020.

developing the self-service check-in kiosk. Jeff has managed to repeatedly achieve success in many verticals. He started out as a software engineer after graduating from Yale University with a computer science degree. His first start-up was a software company he started his freshman year of college to pay his way through college. Jeff is one of the founders of Priceline.com, a company that democratized the sale of travel products such as airplane tickets. He is the founder of multiple start-ups, has been the CEO of both public and private companies, and has served as a senior executive in many capacities.

Jeff has also achieved success in other fields. He is a Hollywood film producer, a producer of a Grammy Award-winning jazz album, and the executive producer of Emmy Award-winning TV show *Success in Your City*. He is also a speaker and published author. Currently, he spends most of his time mentoring youth through Dream Tank, a social entrepreneurship accelerator. Jeff has accomplished enough for multiple lifetimes and was once described "as someone who thrives on turning big problems into even bigger business opportunities" by *Smart Business Magazine*.[98]

When I met Jeff, I asked him how he repeatedly achieved so many life goals. I expected him to tell me he perfected the art of multitasking, but this was not the case. He gave me the analogy of an Olympic athlete who wins a gold medal in a sport. Typically, Olympic athletes do not prepare for multiple sports. For example, you'll rarely find an athlete competing

---

98   Mark Scott, "Jeff Hoffman Thrives on Turning Big Problems into Even Bigger Business Opportunities Such as Priceline.com," *Smart Business*, August 1, 2015.

at the Olympics in multiple disciplines—let's say basketball and swimming—at the same time. Managing the training schedule as well as truly mastering each sport to the point of competing at the highest level, let alone winning a gold medal, would be exceedingly difficult.

Olympic athletes focus on one sport for many years to even get themselves in a position to qualify for the Olympics. Once they have achieved that milestone, they can focus on another goal. Focus is essential if you want to succeed not just in that area, but in others as well.

Jeff went on to explain that he had managed to be successful in multiple fields by focusing on one project at a given time. When he was working on Priceline.com, that was his sole focus and where all his energy was going. Same thing when he was working on the Grammy-winning jazz album. Once he achieved a goal, he would repeat the same process for his next priority goal.

When you have SOS (shiniest object syndrome) and chase every new idea that comes to mind, you will most likely catch none. Lack of focus can easily lead to lack of achievement because you may never apply enough energy on one thing until it is completed. Having an SOS mindset is like playing a game of Whac-A-Mole with your life's goals. The idea of focusing on one thing until it's complete and overcoming SOS is not limited to your goals but also to daily tasks and projects. Focus is key in the entire process.

Many other successful people have used a similar approach. A great example is Jeff Bezos at Amazon. When Jeff Bezos started Amazon in 1994, he focused on selling in one category—books. Initially, Bezos had a list of twenty products he felt had great online potential, but then he narrowed the list to the five most promising product categories: compact discs, computer hardware, computer software, videos, and books.[99] Finally, he landed on books because of the large worldwide demand for literature, the low unit price for books, and the huge number of titles available in print. By focusing on one product category first, Bezos and his team were able to win the "gold medal" for selling books online by becoming the largest online marketplace for books.

In fact, Amazon.com became the first internet retailer to secure one million customers in 1997, the year it went public.[100] From 1994 to 1998, Amazon was an online bookstore. In 1998, it started expanded into other categories, namely music and video. It later expanded to selling toys, electronics, tools, and hardware the year after. As it won more "gold medals," the business kept growing to what we know Amazon to be today: a global tech company focused on e-commerce, cloud computing, digital streaming, artificial intelligence, and whatever else it wants. When you look closely at the Amazon progression, you cannot be faulted for thinking that Bezos applied the S.P.E.A.R. method.

99 "Amazon.com, Inc. History," Funding Universe, accessed April 17, 2020.

100 History.com Editors, "Amazon Opens for Business," HISTORY, A&E Television Networks, November 4, 2015.

YOU CAN'T LIVE OFF YESTERDAY'S VICTORIES
(OR FAILURES)

John Wooden is considered one of the greatest NCAA basketball coaches of all time. As the head coach of UCLA, he won ten NCAA national championships in a twelve-year period, including seven in a row, a feat no other team has managed as of this writing. Wooden often reminded his players to make each day a masterpiece and to not live in the past since it will never change. He encouraged them to focus on today—because, truly, today is the only day that really matters.

So, go ahead and set those grand goals and visions. Take action each day to make sure you reach greater heights than before. Be sure to enjoy the experience—as you know, tomorrow is never guaranteed.

CONCLUSION

———

Whatever the mind can conceive and believe, the mind can achieve.

—NAPOLEON HILL

For ten years, I had been my parent's last-born child. So when they came home from the hospital with my younger sister, Jane, I was excited to meet her. I remember that the first time I held her, she was so tiny and adorable. As I cradled her in my arms, I noticed both her hands were clenched into fists. I asked my mother why babies do that, and she said because they are holding on to their life's gifts. In that moment, I realized we are all born with a set of unique gifts and that each of our lives has a specific purpose.

Ralph Waldo Emerson once said, "To be yourself in a world that is constantly trying to make you something else is the greatest accomplishment." That is why you need to make sure you invest the time to **seek your why**: your life's purpose, the reason you were born. Without knowing your purpose, you risk leading a directionless life—a life without meaning and nothing to aim for. Such a life does not make you feel "alive." Zig Ziglar famously said, "If you aim at nothing, you will hit it every time."

With this clarity, you can create a **plan** on how you will achieve your purpose. Break down your why into goals you will achieve over the course of your "bus ride."

A plan will do you no good if you do not **execute** the plan. Through relentless execution, you will achieve your goals. Since each goal is a stepping-stone to your life's purpose, **repeat** the process until you achieve your life's purpose.

Throughout mankind's history, we have seen how tools have improved our way of life. The spear changed the game. This simple yet effective tool not only drastically improved man's chances of survival but even allowed man to thrive. Just as the spear positively transformed life for ancient mankind, the S.P.E.A.R. method is that transformative tool for modern day mankind.

So even when you have just achieved the biggest goal humankind has ever seen achieved, you now have a chance to set a new one to pursue. Dream big in all areas of life and let the S.P.E.A.R. method help you get there.

Please do not forget to check out *www.SPEARMethod.com*—my team and I created so many FREE resources you can use to help you throughout the process, and you can find out how to connect with me directly, if you would like to. Plus, you can download a BONUS CHAPTER.

Go out there and enjoy the *hunt*.

Thanks,
Kuda Biza

PS Don't forget, you are only one goal away . . .

BIBLIOGRAPHY

———

INTRODUCTION

Cohut, Maria. "COVID-19 Global Impact: How the Coronavirus Is Affecting the World." *Medical News Today,* April 24, 2020. *https://www.medicalnewstoday.com/articles/covid-19-global-impact-how-the-coronavirus-is-affecting-the-world.*

Lee, Don. "Unemployment Hits 14.7% in April. How Long before 20.5 Million Lost Jobs Come Back?" *LA Times,* May 8, 2020. *https://www.latimes.com/politics/story/2020-05-08/jobs-report-labor-market-shock.*

Samukange, Tinotenda. "Rabid Dog Leaves 3 Dead, 13 Injured." *News Day,* May 15, 2015. *https://www.newsday.co.zw/2015/05/rabid-dog-leaves-3-dead-13-injured/.*

CHAPTER 1

National Museum Publications. "Weapons of Southern Africa." Accessed May 24, 2020. *https://nationalmuseumpublications.co.za/weapons-of-southern-africa.*

Poirier, Corey. "Why Your 'Why' Matters." *Forbes*, October 31, 2017. https://www.forbes.com/sites/forbescoachescouncil/2017/10/31/why-your-why-matters/#7457769856b5.

Ratner, Ben. "3 Key Marketing Takeaways from Simon Sinek's "Start with Why."" *Hubspot* (blog). October 29, 2019. https://blog.hubspot.com/customers/3-takeaways-from-start-with-why.

CHAPTER 2

Merriam-Webster. s.v. "curiosity (_n._)." Accessed April 6, 2020. https://www.merriam-webster.com/dictionary/curiosity.

UNESCO. "263 Million Children and Youth Are Out Of School | UNESCO UIS." UNESCO News. Accessed on January 22, 2020. *http://uis.unesco.org/en/news/263-million-children-and-youth-are-out-school.*

White House. "Champions of Change—Joshua Williams." Accessed February 6, 2020. https://obamawhitehouse.archives.gov/champions/strengthening-food-security/joshua-williams.

CHAPTER 3

Burke, Andrew, Stuart Fraser, and Francis J. Greene. "The Multiple Effects Of Business Planning On New Venture Performance." *Journal of Management Studies* 47, 3 (2010): 391-415. doi:10.1111/j.1467-6486.2009.00857.x.

PR Newswire. "Survey Finds Two-Thirds of Americans Do Not Have a Plan for Their Life." Accessed March 7, 2020. *https://www.prnewswire.com/news-releases/survey-finds-two-thirds-of-americans-do-not-have-a-plan-for-their-life-300564102.html.*

Zigler, Travis and Jenna Zigler. "Creating A Vivid Vision." July 27, 2018. #ThisIsMyEra the Podcast. Produced by Kuda Biza and

Alexander Star. Podcast, MP3 Audio, 44:04. *https://thisismyera.com/blogs/podcast/ep7-eyelove.*

CHAPTER 4

Makura, Moky. "Nigel Chanakira—The Wonder Boy Entrepreneur." In Africa's Greatest Entrepreneurs, 142–60. Cape Town: Penguin, 2008.

Perry, Mark. "Fortune 500 firms in 1955 vs. 2014; 88% are gone, and we're all better off because of that dynamic 'creative destruction'" *AEI* (blog). August 18, 2014. *https://www.aei.org/carpe-diem/fortune-500-firms-in-1955-vs-2014-89-are-gone-and-were-all-better-off-because-of-that-dynamic-creative-destruction/.*

ThisIsMyEra LLC. *#ThisIsMyEra 90-Day Planner* (Florida: ThisIsMyEra LLC, 2017), 4-5.

CHAPTER 5

Higher Life Foundation. "About Us." Accessed April 26, 2020. *https://www.higherlifefoundation.com/about-us/.*

Higher Life Foundation. "Home Page." Accessed April 26, 2020. *https://www.higherlifefoundation.com/.*

Makura, Moky. "Strive Masiyiwa—The Spiritual Entrepreneur." In Africa's Greatest Entrepreneurs, 82–106. Cape Town: Penguin, 2008.

McMenamin, Dave. "For the Cavaliers, There's A King and There's A Champ." *ESPN.com,* December 15, 2015. *https://www.espn.com/nba/story/_/id/14373719/lebron-james-james-jones-unique-bond.*

National Center for Education Statistics. "Tuition Costs of Colleges and Universities." Accessed March 12, 2020. *https://nces.ed.gov/ fastfacts/display.asp?id=76*.

National Collegiate Athletic Association. "Estimated Probability of Competing in College Athletics." Accessed January 3, 2020. *http://www.ncaa.org/about/resources/research/estimated-probability-competing-college-athletics*.

National Collegiate Athletic Association. "Estimated Probability of Competing in Professional Athletics." Accessed January 3, 2020. *http://www.ncaa.org/about/resources/research/estimated-probability-competing-professional-athletics*.

The World Bank. "GDP per Capital (Current US$)—Zimbabwe." Accessed May 27, 2020. *https://data.worldbank.org/indicator/ NY.GDP.PCAP.CD?locations=ZW*.

U.S. Embassy in Zimbabwe. "Educational Advising." Accessed June 2, 2020. *https://zw.usembassy.gov/education-culture/educational-advising/*.

CHAPTER 6

Clear, James. "How to Build New Habits: This Is Your Strategy Guide." Accessed March 6, 2020 *https://jamesclear.com/habit-guide*.

Davis, Scott. "Michael Jordan Once Added 15 Pounds of Muscle In One Summer To Prepare For A Rival And Changed The Way Athletes Train." *Insider.com*, April 27, 2020. *https://www.insider. com/michael-jordan-trained-15-pounds-muscle-pistons-2020-4*.

Jordan, Michael. *The Last Dance*. Episode 8, "Episode VIII." Directed by Jason Hehir. Aired May 10, 2020, on ESPN.

Lehrer, Jonah. "Blame It on the Brain." *Wall Street Journal*, December 6, 2009. *https://www.wsj.com/articles/SB10001424052748703 478704574612052322122442.*

Martin, Rover. "The Execution Trap." *Harvard Business Review* (July/August 2010). *https://hbr.org/2010/07/the-execution-trap.*

Money Chimp. "Simple Interest Calculator." Accessed February 21, 2020. *http://www.moneychimp.com/features/simple_interest_calculator.htm.*

National Hockey League. "NHL Hart Memorial Trophy Winners." Accessed April 13, 2020. *https://www.nhl.com/news/nhl-hart-memorial-trophy-winners-complete-list/c-287743272.*

National Hockey League. "Skater Records—Most Goals, Career." Accessed April 13, 2020. *https://records.nhl.com/records/skater-records/goals/most-goals-career.*

Norcross, John C., Marci S. Mrykalo, and Matthew D. Blagys. "Auld Lang Syne: Success Predictors, Change Processes, and Self-Reported Outcomes of New Year's Resolvers and Nonresolvers." *Journal of Clinical Psychology* 58, 4 (2002): 397–405. *https://doi.org/https://doi.org/10.1002/jclp.1151.*

CHAPTER 7

Quandt, Katie Rose. "Who Gets to Be A Risk Taker?" *Headspace* (blog). Accessed March 6, 2020. *https://www.headspace.com/blog/2017/09/28/risk-taker/.*

World Health Organization. "Global Status Report on Road Safety 2018." Accessed February 16, 2020. *https://www.who.int/publications/i/item/global-status-report-on-road-safety-2018.*

CHAPTER 8

American Psychological Association. "Stress in America: Our Health at Risk." Accessed March 12, 2020. *http://www.apa.org/news/press/releases/stress/2011/final-2011.pdf.*

Cohen, Jennifer. "5 Proven Methods for Gaining Self Discipline." *Forbes*, June 18, 2014. *https://www.forbes.com/sites/jennifer-cohen/2014/06/18/5-proven-methods-for-gaining-self-discipline/#4dbde67d3c9f.*

De Ridder, Denise T.D., Gerty Lensvelt-Mulders, Catrin Finkenauer, F. Marijn Stok, and Roy F. Baumeister. 2012. "Taking Stock of Self-Control: A Meta-Analysis of How Trait Self-Control Relates to a Wide Range of Behaviors." *Personality and Social Psychology Review* 16 (1): 76–99. *https://doi.org/https://doi.org/10.1177/1088868311418749.*

Diaz, Cheyenne. "The Staggering Power of Self Talk On The Body And Mind" *MindValley* (blog). January 23, 2018. *https://blog.mindvalley.com/self-talk/.*

Elrod, Hal. "The 5-Step Snooze-Proof Wake Up Strategy." *The Miracle Morning*, 44–45. Hal Elrod International Inc., 2016.

Lexico. s.v. "self-discipline (_n._)." Accessed May 6, 2020. *https://www.lexico.com/en/definition/self-discipline.*

Merriam-Webster. s.v. "courage (_n._)." Accessed April 11, 2020. *https://www.merriam-webster.com/dictionary/courage.*

Merriam-Webster. s.v. "self-discipline (_n._)." Accessed May 9, 2020. *https://www.merriam-webster.com/dictionary/self-discipline.*

Penner, Mike. "U.S. Gymnast Braves Pain for Gold." *LA Times*, July 24, 1996. *https://www.latimes.com/archives/la-xpm-1996-07-24-mn-27396-story.html.*

Wolchover, Natalie. "Why Do People Take Risks?" *Live Science.* August 30, 2011. *https://www.livescience.com/33471-people-take-risks.html.*

CHAPTER 9

Alhola, Paula, and Paivi Polo-Kantola. "Sleep Deprivation: Impact on Cognitive Performance." *Neuropsychiatric Disease and Treatment* 3 (5): 553–67. Accessed May 6, 2020. *https://www.ncbi.nlm.nih.gov/pmc/articles/PMC2656292/.*

Booktable. "Why We Sleep: Unlocking the Power of Sleep and Dreams." Accessed May 14, 2020. *https://www.booktable.net/book/9781501144318.*

Delle, Sangu. "Home Page." Accessed January 5, 2020. *http://www.sdelle.com/.*

Elrod, Hal. *The Miracle Morning.* Hal Elrod International Inc., 2016.

Golden Palm Investments. "Responsibility." Accessed January 3, 2020. *https://www.gpalminvestments.com/responsibility.*

Hole, Kori. "Andela's $700 Million Valuation Puts Africa's Tech Ecosystem at Risk." *Forbes,* Oct 3, 2019. *https://www.forbes.com/sites/korihale/2019/10/03/andelas-700-million-valuation-puts-africas-tech-ecosystem-at-risk/#c04bb9b2c4c7.*

Hughes, Locke. "I tried the 'The Miracle Morning' productivity routine for a month. Here's what happened." *NBC News,* March 17, 2019. *https://www.nbcnews.com/better/lifestyle/i-tried-miracle-morning-routine-month-here-s-what-happened-ncna981786.*

Lufkin, Bryan. "Is waking up early good or bad?" *BBC,* February 13, 2019. *https://www.bbc.com/worklife/article/20190213-is-waking-up-early-good-or-bad.*

Mooventhan, A., and L. Nivethitha. "Scientific Evidence-Based Effects of Hydrotherapy on Various Systems of the Body," *North American Journal of Medical Sciences*, 199–209. Accessed March 9, 2020. *https:/dx.doi.org/10.4103/1947-2714.132935.*

National Heart, Lung, and Blood Institute. "Sleep Deprivation and Deficiency." Accessed May 8, 2020. *https://www.nhlbi.nih.gov/health-topics/sleep-deprivation-and-deficiency.*

Nutt, David, Sue Wilson, and Louise Paterson. "Sleep Disorders as Core Symptoms of Depression." *Dialogues in Clinical Neuroscience* 10 (3): 329–36. Accessed May 13, 2020. *https://www.ncbi.nlm.nih.gov/pmc/articles/PMC3181883/.*

Saltuary. "Sleep—The New Wonder Pill for Health and Happiness." Accessed May 10, 2020. *https://saltuary.com.au/sleep-the-new-wonder-pill-for-health-and-happiness/.*

Society for Neuroscience. "Scientists Find Brain Areas Affected By Lack Of Sleep." *ScienceDaily*. Accessed May 16, 2020. *www.sciencedaily.com/releases/2003/11/031113065511.htm.*

Szegedy-Maszak, Marianne. "Mysteries of The Mind." Auburn University. Accessed March 25, 2020. *http://webhome.auburn.edu/~mitrege/ENGL2210/USNWR-mind.html.*

Wim Hof Method. "Benefits." Accessed January 14, 2020. *https://www.wimhofmethod.com/benefits.*

CHAPTER 10

Callagy Law. "Sean Callagy." Accessed June 1, 2020. *https://callagylaw.com/attorneys/sean-callagy-esq/.*

Conversano, Ciro, Alessandro Rotondo, Elena Lensi, Olivia D. Vista, Francesca Arpone, and Mario A. Reda. "Optimism and Its Impact on Mental and Physical Well-Being." *Clinical*

Practice and Epidemiology in Mental Health Vol. 6 (May 2010): 25-29. *https://doi.org/10.2174/1745017901006010025*.

Digitale, Erin. "Positive attitude toward math predicts math achievement in kids." *Stanford University Medicine News*. January 24, 2018. *http://med.stanford.edu/news/all-news/2018/01/positive-attitude-toward-math-predicts-math-achievement-in-kids.html*.

International Association for the Study of Lung Cancer. "Lung cancer patients with optimistic attitudes have longer survival, study finds." *ScienceDaily*. Accessed May 12, 2020. *https://www.sciencedaily.com/releases/2010/03/100303131656.htm*.

Khan Academy. "Newton's Third Law of Motion." Accessed April 27, 2020. *https://www.khanacademy.org/science/physics/forces-newtons-laws/newtons-laws-of-motion/v/newton-s-third-law-of-motion*.

Meevissen, Yvo M.C., Madelon L. Peters, and Hugo J.E.M. Alberts. "Become More Optimistic by Imagining a Best Possible Self: Effects of a Two Week Intervention." *Journal of Behavior Therapy and Experimental Psychiatry* 42, 3 (September 2011): 371–78. *https://doi.org/10.1016/j.jbtep.2011.02.012*.

Reierson, Timothy. "Attitude to Succeed." *Accountancy Student Blog* (blog). College of Business at Illinois. April 22, 2016. *http://blogs.business.illinois.edu/accountancy-students/attitude-to-succeed/*.

Segerstrom, Suzanne C. "How Does Optimism Suppress Immunity? Evaluation of Three Affective Pathways." *Health Psychology*, 25, 5 (September 2006): 653–657. *https://doi.org/10.1037/0278-6133.25.5.653*.

Seligman, Martin E, and Peter Schulman. "Explanatory Style as a Predictor of Productivity and Quitting Among Life Insurance Sales Agents." *Journal of Personality and Social Psychology* 50(4) (1986): 832–838. *https://doi.org/10.1037/0022-3514.50.4.832.*

Selk, Jason. "7 Ways to Become A More Optimistic Person." Mindbodygreen. Accessed May 7, 2020. *https://www.mindbodygreen. com/0-7949/7-ways-to-become-a-more-optimistic-person.html.*

Warrell, Margie. "See the Glass Half Full Or Empty? Why Optimists Are Happier, Healthier & Wealthier!" *Forbes.* September 29, 2012. *https://www.forbes.com/sites/margiewarrell/2012/09/19/ see-the-glass-half-empty-or-full-7-keys-for-optimism-in-tough-times/#70c9e1e8767f.*

CHAPTER 11

Carr, Priyanka, and Gregory Walton. "Cues of Working Together Fuel Intrinsic Motivation." *Journal of Experimental Social Psychology* 53 (July 2014): 169–84. *https://doi.org/https://doi. org/10.1016/j.jesp.2014.03.015.*

D'Onfro, Jillian. "Mark Zuckerberg says that visiting an Indian temple at the urging of Steve Jobs helped him stick to Facebook's mission." *Business Insider.* September 27, 2015. *https:// www.businessinsider.com/mark-zuckerberg-visited-india-thanks-to-steve-jobs-2015-9.*

Gaskell, Adi. "New Study Finds That Collaboration Drives Workplace Performance." *Forbes.* June 22, 2017. *https://www.forbes. com/sites/adigaskell/2017/06/22/new-study-finds-that-collaboration-drives-workplace-performance/#56742c063d02.*

John, Elton. "Elton John." Accessed March 13, 2020. *https://www. eltonjohn.com/elton-john.*

Jude, Joseph. "Network Like A Pro." Accessed April 27, 2020. *https://www.jjude.com/network-like-pro.*

Krohn, Kris. "Mentors are the most important key to success…" Facebook, May 21, 2020. *https://www.facebook.com/Mentor-withKris/posts/531503337525565.*

Macchio, Ralph, and Noriyuki Morita. *The Karate Kid.* VHS. Directed by John Avildsen. United States: Columbia Pictures, 1984.

Moseley, Corey. "7 reasons why collaboration is important." *Jostle* (blog). Accessed May 3, 2020. *https://blog.jostle.me/blog/why-collaboration-is-important.*

Oppong, Thomas. "Psychological Secrets to Hack Your Way to Better Life Habits." *Observer.* March 20, 2017. *https://observer.com/2017/03/psychological-secrets-hack-better-life-habits-psychology-productivity/.*

Osho, Samuel. "5 Powerful Mentoring Relationships that Influenced the World." *Samosho* (blog). August 12, 2018. *https://www.samosho.com/5-powerful-mentoring-relationships-that-influenced-the-world/.*

Procter & Gamble. "Annual Report 2019." Accessed May 6, 2020. *https://www.pg.com/annualreport2019/index.html#/.*

Procter & Gamble. "Company History." Accessed May 6, 2020. *https://www.pg.com/en_US/downloads/media/Fact_Sheets_CompanyHistory.pdf.*

Rapp, Alyssa. "Be One, Get One: The Importance of Mentorship." *Forbes.* October 2, 2018. *https://www.forbes.com/sites/yec/2018/10/02/be-one-get-one-the-importance-of-mentorship/#1e3676b17434.*

Triffin, Molly. "8 Secrets from Power Networking Pros." *Forbes.* July 23, 2014. *https://www.forbes.com/sites/learnvest/2014/07/23/secrets-from-power-networking-pros/#25bb632b4e5a.*

United Nations. "Sustainable Development—Education." Accessed March 12, 2020. *https://www.un.org/sustainabledevelopment/education/.*

CHAPTER 12

Chu, Melissa. "Sylvester Stallone on fighting for what you want." *The Ladders.* April 10, 2020. *https://www.theladders.com/career-advice/sylvester-stallone-on-fighting-for-what-you-want.*

National Center for Education Statistics. "Tuition Costs of Colleges and Universities." Accessed March 12, 2020. *https://nces.ed.gov/fastfacts/display.asp?id=76.*

The Numbers. "Rocky." Accessed May 3, 2020. *https://www.the-numbers.com/movies/franchise/Rocky#tab=summary.*

US Inflation Calculator. "Current US Inflation Rates: 2009-2020." Accessed June 2, 2020. *https://www.usinflationcalculator.com/inflation/current-inflation-rates/#:~:text=The%20annual%20inflation%20rate%20for,published%20on%20May%2012%2C%202020.*

Ward, Tom. "The Amazing Story of The Making Of 'Rocky.'" *Forbes.* August 29, 2017. *https://www.forbes.com/sites/tomward/2017/08/29/the-amazing-story-of-the-making-of-rocky/#b-fb2e95560bb.*

World Data. "Development of inflation rates in Zimbabwe." Accessed June 2, 2020. *https://www.worlddata.info/africa/zimbabwe/inflation-rates.php.*

CHAPTER 13

Cordes Foundation. "Ron Cordes: How to Make Your Second Career Count." Accessed May 29, 2020. *https://cordesfounda-*

tion.org/2015/08/24/ron-cordes-how-to-make-your-second-career-count/.

Cordes Foundation. "Solving the World's Problems." Accessed May 29, 2020. *https://cordesfoundation.org/2014/05/02/solving-the-worlds-problems/.*

Encyclopaedia Britannica Online. s.v. "Cellular Respiration." Accessed April 6, 2020, *https://www.britannica.com/science/cellular-respiration.*

Fairchild, Caroline. "How Ron Cordes Went from Profits to Purpose." *Fortune*, April 11, 2014. *https://fortune.com/2014/04/11/how-ron-cordes-went-from-profits-to-purpose/.*

Funding Universe. "Amazon.com, Inc. History." Accessed April 17, 2020. *http://www.fundinguniverse.com/company-histories/amazon-com-inc-history/.*

History.com Editors. "Amazon Opens for Business." *HISTORY, A&E Television Networks.* November 4, 2015. *https://www.history.com/this-day-in-history/amazon-opens-for-business.*

Khan Academy. "Cellular Respiration." Accessed April 27, 2020. *https://www.khanacademy.org/science/high-school-biology/hs-energy-and-transport/hs-cellular-respiration/a/hs-cellular-respiration-review.*

Scott, Mark. "Jeff Hoffman Thrives on Turning Big Problems into Even Bigger Business Opportunities Such as Priceline.com." *Smart Business.* August 1, 2015. *https://www.sbnonline.com/article/jeff-hoffman-thrives-on-turning-big-problems-into-even-bigger-business-opportunities-such-as-priceline-com/.*

Wildermuth, Erin. "The Science of Celebration: 5 Reasons Organizations Should Do It More Often." *Michael Hyatt* (blog). Accessed May 13, 2020. *https://michaelhyatt.com/science-of-celebration/.*

ACKNOWLEDGEMENTS

In Africa, we say it takes a village to raise a child, and the same is true for this book. I would like to thank my "village" that has helped me write this book.

I must start by thanking my beautiful and amazing wife, Ruth. From reading early drafts of the book to helping with the book cover design and all the date nights we missed so I could edit, she was as important to this book getting done as I was. #Always&Forever! Thank you so much, my love.

To Mum and Dad, thank you for the constant unconditional love and support. Thank you for seeing the potential in me even when I was unable to. For all the sacrifices that you made for me—I am forever grateful.

To my sisters—Martha, Miriam, and Jane—thank you for knowing the right things to say at the right time. Your messages kept me going throughout this process.

Thank you to everyone I interviewed. I am grateful for your taking time out of your busy schedules to talk to me and share your wisdom. This book would not have been the same without your insights.

To my "right-hand" lady, Melissa DeLay, to whom I'm forever indebted, thank you for the editorial help, keen insight, and ongoing support in bringing my visions to life.

A HUGE thank to the New Degree Press team—you guys rock. Special thanks to Eric Koester, Brian Bies, Linda Berardelli, Alexander Pyles, Casey Mahalik, and Gjorgji Pejkovski.

I would like to personally thank the people at AFR Clothing, #ThisIsMyEra, Signables, Amani Hope Foundation, and Nunbelievable. Teamwork truly makes the dream work, and you are all wonderful people who have already made a lot of dreams come true. Let's keep pushing and make millions more dreams a reality.

To everyone who supported my pre-launch campaign, THANK YOU: Lauren Cecchi, Danene Jaffe, Asoka Veeravagu, Jose Lopez, Dalumuzi Mhlanga, Scott Tennant, Harriet Donkor, Precious Chifunyise, Nicholas Haggarty, Kelvin Kaura, David Tswamuno, Aubrey Magodlyo, Lauren Kester, Ato Eyiah, Lauren Siclare, Joel Julio, John Giarratano, Cyan Bonacci, Itayi Chibaya, David Matsekeza, Ryan S. Feigenblatt, Pedro Moras, James Colclough, David M. Baldwin, Andrew Shell, Ingrid Fraser, Pam Luckie, Ronald Terpilowski, Devon Baltrus, and Team Canada.

To Alexander Star, my brother from another mother, THANK YOU for always inspiring me to make it my ERA! I am always encouraged by your unwavering pursuit of your why. I took inspiration from that as I was writing this book.

Saving the best for last—I want to thank God most of all, because without God I wouldn't be able to do any of this.

ABOUT THE AUTHOR

Kuda Biza is a serial entrepreneur who started his first company when he was nine years old in Zimbabwe. Kuda moved to the United States with only $40 in his pocket to study at Lynn University, where he started his second company. Kuda then spent over a decade in various roles at a Fortune 500 company responsible for launching multimillion-dollar strategic new growth initiatives. Kuda also cofounded Nunbelievable, a socially conscious baked goods company, as well as a personal development company and a sports collectibles company, and launched a fashion brand in the Middle East.

Kuda believes in being a force of good and founded the Amani Hope Foundation, a 501(c)(3) nonprofit organization with a mission to empower underprivileged children. When not giving back to communities or working hard in the business world, Kuda can be found cheering on Chelsea FC and spending time with his wife, Ruth.

BONUS CHAPTER

I wrote a bonus chapter just for you
and you can download it for FREE
at the link below:

WWW.SPEARMETHOD.COM/BONUS